REDEEMING OUR REGRETS:

THE ENTANGLED LIVES OF SARAH AND HAGAR

GENE & ELAINE GETZ

Redeeming Our Regrets: The Entangled Lives of Sarah and Hagar
© 2007 Gene and Elaine Getz

Published by Serendipity House Publishers
Nashville, Tennessee

ISBN: 1-5749-4231-X
Dewey Decimal Classification: 248.843
Subject Headings:
CHRISTIAN LIFE \ WOMEN \ WOMEN IN THE BIBLE

Scripture quotations marked HCSB taken from the *Holman Christian Standard Bible®*, Copyright © 1999, 2000, 2002, 2003 by Holman Bible Publishers. Used by permission.

Scriptures marked NASB from the *New American Standard Bible®*, © 1960, 1962, 1963, 1968, 1971, 1972, 1973, 1975, 1977, 1995 by the Lockman Foundation. Used by permission.

Scriptures marked NIV taken from the *Holy Bible, New International Version*, Copyright © 1973, 1978, 1984 by International Bible Society. Used by permission.

Scriptures marked MSG taken from the *THE MESSAGE*, Copyright © 1993, 1994, 1995, 1996, 2000, 2001, 2002. Used by permission of NavPress Publishing Group.

Scriptures marked NLT taken from the *The Holy Bible, New Living Translation*, Copyright © 1996. Used by permission of Tyndale House Publishers, Inc. Wheaton, IL 60189, USA. All rights reserved.

To purchase additional copies of this resource or other studies:
ORDER ONLINE at www.SerendipityHouse.com;
WRITE Serendipity House, 117 10th Avenue North, Nashville, TN 37234
FAX (615) 277-8181 ~ PHONE (800) 525-9563

SERENDIPITY® HOUSE

1-800-525-9563
www.SerendipityHouse.com

Printed in the United States of America
13 12 11 10 09 08 07   1 2 3 4 5 6 7 8 9 10

CONTENTS

SESSION	TITLE	PAGE

LEADER'S GUIDE

Redeeming Our Regrets

HOME...WORKS
MARRIAGE & FAMILY SERIES

**Check these and other great studies
at www.SerendipityHouse.com ...**

Some Assembly Required: Instructions for an Amazing Marriage

Dream Team: The Power of Two

Turning Up the Heat: Rekindle Romance and Passion

Coauthoring Your Child's Story: Parenting on Purpose

Can You Hear Me Now?: Communication in Marriage

Creating Mutual Funds: Financial Teamwork in Marriage

CREDITS

Serendipity House along with Gene and Elaine Getz wish to thank
Regal Books, friends and partners in ministry, for graciously granting
permission to include content from Gene and Elaine's book *The
Measure of a Woman* in this Women of Purpose series.

Redeeming Our Regrets

REDEEMING OUR REGRETS

THE ENTANGLED LIVES OF
SARAH AND HAGAR

The Entangled Lives of Sarah and Hagar sounds like a soap opera, and the lives of these women reads like a soap opera. Sarah is the wife of a wealthy man, and Hagar is Sarah's servant. Both are the kind of women to whom we all can relate. They made mistakes, they repeated their mistakes, they struggled through difficult times in life, and they knew what it felt like to fail.

The turning point in this story is when God entangles Himself into both of their lives. Both women had regrets, by God in His intense love made Sarah the mother of a great nation, His chosen people, the Jews. In the same way, He mercifully rescued Hagar from death and made her the mother of another great nation, the Ishmaelites. Like these women, you too can find redemption from the regrets that seem to haunt you, and experience the deep joy and peace that comes from truly seeing "the God who sees" you!

Redeeming Our Regrets is a unique study for women, which blends fun elements, interactive discovery-focused Bible study, creative experiential activities, and wonderful opportunities to connect with God, with other women, and with your heart. Journal pages are provided with each session to support you in taking some of your deepest longings and questions to your heart and to God. Take the rocky path of redemption with Sarah and Hagar.

* At the Crossroads of Fear and Faith – strengthening faith and beliefs
* Déjà Vu All Over Again – getting out of our ruts
* Large and In Charge – embracing pain and crying out to God
* God Comes Through ... Plus Some – receiving God's best
* The Rollercoaster Ride of Emotions – seeing with new eyes
* Streams in the Desert – staying in the journey and finishing strong

The Women of Purpose series highlights ordinary women used by God in extraordinary ways. As we delve below the surface and into the hearts of these women, we discover not only who they are, but also who *we* are. We find our hearts awakening to deeper intimacy with God and to an increasing desire to give ourselves to something grand, noble, and bigger than ourselves. We don't have to settle for simply existing; God created us to really live—to be women of passion and women of purpose.

AT THE CROSSROADS OF FEAR AND FAITH

From the first moments of creation in Genesis to the last triumphant promise recorded in Revelation, God continually works in the business of redemption. He brings light out of darkness, order out of chaos, hope out of despair, and life out of death. We often forget that our God really can do *anything*. The stories recorded in the Bible are tender reminders that God comes to the rescue of weak, imperfect people to bring to completion His ultimate act of redemption—the creation of a new earth and a new heaven in which Jesus can live forever with His people—His bride.

BREAKING THE ICE - *10-15 Minutes*

LEADER: These "Breaking the Ice" experiences are designed to get people talking. Encourage each group member to participate, but be sure to keep things moving. The activity helps get group members acquainted with one another. Pass out paper, pens, colored markers, and crayons.

1. Write your first name vertically along the left margin of a sheet of paper. Using the letters of your first name, create an acrostic that describes you. For instance:

   E nthusiastic about gardening
   M other of four children
   I nterested in politics and current events
   L oves Italian food
   Y earns to hike the Appalachian Trail

2. Decorate your acrostic by drawing pictures that also identify something about you.

3. Share your acrostic with the group. Then, as others share, try to memorize at least one new thing about each of the other group members.

DISCOVERING THE TRUTH
30-35 Minutes

LEADER: For "Discovering the Truth," ask various group members to read the Bible passages aloud. Be sure to leave time for the "Embracing the Truth" and "Connecting" segments that follow this discussion.

EXPLORING OUR EMPTY PLACES

Two women who experienced God's redeeming power in intimate and life-changing ways were Sarah (who begins our study with the name Sarai) and Hagar. Sarah, the wife of a wealthy man, thinks the greatest blessings in life have passed her by. When God calls her husband to a new country and gives him a spectacular promise, she finds her life turned upside down. Hagar, a woman forced to play a role in Sarah's story, is an Egyptian slave. In their entangled lives, both women experience tragedies because of pride and lack of trust in God. But God does not allow their stories to end there.

We first meet Sarai in Genesis 11:27-31. In these four short verses, we learn vital things about Sarai that give us a revealing glimpse into her life.

²⁷ These are the family records of Terah. Terah fathered Abram, Nahor, and Haran, and Haran fathered Lot. ... ²⁹ Abram and Nahor took wives: Abram's wife was named Sarai, and Nahor's wife was named Milcah. ... ³⁰ Sarai was barren; she had no child. ³¹ Terah took his son Abram, his grandson Lot (Haran's son), and his daughter-in-law Sarai, his son Abram's wife, and they set out together from Ur of the Chaldeans to go to the land of Canaan. But when they came to Haran, they settled there.

GENESIS 11:27, 29-31, HCSB

LEADER: Discuss as many discovery questions as time permits. Encourage participation by inviting different individuals to respond. It will help to highlight in advance the questions you don't want to miss. Be familiar with the Scripture Notes at the end of this session.

1. Names of people and places hold significant meaning in the Bible. Judging by Sarai's name (which means "princess"), to what sort of lifestyle might she be accustomed? What sort of expectations do you assume she may have had for her life?

The first revealing thing we notice about Sarai is her name, which means "my princess." With it come connotations of royalty, privilege, strength, independence, and even stubbornness. Another significant fact is that Sarai and Abram are half siblings; Sarai is the daughter of Terah and a different wife. This was a common practice in ancient times, and it will become an important point as the story unfolds.

2. With what significant issue is Sarai struggling (verse 30)? Do you know anyone who has struggled with infertility? How did the struggle affect that person's identity? Relationship with God? Relationship with others?

3. In Sarai's day, a woman's identity and status were measured by her ability to bear offspring. How is a woman's status or identity established in our culture? In what ways do we tell women that they are not "measuring up" as women?

In ancient times, barrenness was considered a shameful, possibly even a God-forsaken, state for a woman. Sarai had no greater purpose in that time and place than to raise children and carry on the family name, a purpose she had little hope of fulfilling.

4. Barrenness was the key, defining trait for Sarai. How would you expect her barrenness to affect her emotions? How about her perceptions of herself, God, and other people?

In his book *The Mystery of Love*, Rabbi Marc Gafni shares the one lesson that he most emphasizes to his students: "Life is what you do with your emptiness." [1] Emptiness, as we will see, presented a defining problem for Sarai—just as it does for millions today. All people experience emptiness and seek to fill it. God, speaking in metaphor, highlights two approaches we can take ...

"For My people have committed a double evil: They have abandoned Me, the fountain of living water, and dug cisterns for themselves, cracked cisterns that cannot hold water."

JEREMIAH 2:13, HCSB

5. What do the cisterns in Jeremiah 2:13 represent? What happens when we fall into relying on our own resources rather than taking our emptiness and deepest thirsts to God?

[35] Jesus said, "I am the Bread of Life. The person who aligns with me hungers no more and thirsts no more, ever. [36] I have told you this explicitly because even though you have seen me in action, you really don't believe me. [37] Every person the Father gives me eventually comes running to me. And once that person is with me, I hold on and don't let go.

JOHN 6:35-37, THE MESSAGE

6. What are the results Jesus promises in John 6 if we take our heart needs and emptiness to Him? How does His offer differ from those things to which people typically turn to fill those empty places?

At times, our arms feel empty, our work feels empty, our relationships feel empty. Too often, we choose to deny the emptiness, or we try to fill it with unsatisfying substitutes. The course of our lives depends largely on this choice of how to fill our emptiness. And, as we'll see in Sarai's case, some attempts to fill it prove far more successful than others.

Session One

Principle for Living

As you acknowledge and explore the empty places in your heart, you'll begin to recognize the deepest desires and thirsts you long to satisfy. Embracing Jesus and His living water is the only thing that will ever fill your empty places.

STANDING AT A CROSSROADS

Sarai, her husband, Abram, and extended family had recently moved from Ur of the Chaldeans to Haran, a region whose name literally means "crossroads." In Haran, God visited Abram and challenged him with Sarai and take a great step of faith into the unknown.

LEADER: Invite two or three volunteers to divide the reading of Genesis 12.

¹ The LORD said to Abram: Go out from your land, your relatives, and your father's house to the land that I will show you. ² I will make you into a great nation, I will bless you, I will make your name great, and you will be a blessing. ³ I will bless those who bless you, I will curse those who treat you with contempt, and all the peoples on earth will be blessed through you.

⁴ So Abram went, as the LORD had told him, and Lot went with him. Abram was 75 years old when he left Haran. ⁵ He took his wife Sarai, his nephew Lot, all the possessions they had accumulated, and the people he had acquired in Haran, and they set out for the land of Canaan. When they came to the land of Canaan, ⁶ Abram passed through the land to the site of Shechem, at the oak of Moreh. At that time the Canaanites were in the land. ⁷ But the LORD appeared to Abram and said, "I will give this land to your offspring." So he built an altar there to the LORD who had appeared to him.

⁸ From there he moved on to the hill country east of Bethel and pitched his tent, with Bethel on the west and Ai on the east. There he built an altar to the LORD and worshiped Him. ⁹ Then Abram journeyed by stages to the Negev.

GENESIS. 12:1-9, HCSB

Bible scholar John MacArthur tells us that the journey from Ur to Haran would have been around 700 miles, and the journey from Haran to Canaan totaled around 350 miles. Abram's caravan was large, including Sarai, Abram's nephew Lot, and all the menservants and maidservants and animals that were part of a wealthy man's estate.² To Sarai fell the responsibility of overseeing the caravan and maintaining the "household" as they traveled these many miles.

7. What were the key elements of God's vision for Abram (verses 1-3)? How, specifically, do you think God's vision would affect Sarai?

8. Given Sarai's barrenness and advanced age, how do you suppose she would have responded to Abram's report about God's promises to him?

9. Why do you think God withholds from us complete, detailed outlines of our futures? What benefit is there in asking us to "live by faith, not by sight" (2 Corinthians 5:7, NIV)?

Principle for Living

When you reach a life crossroads, it's easy to give in to fear. Remember decisions based on fear are almost always regrettable because fear blinds us to the opportunities and blessings God plans for us.

Decades passed before Abram and Sarai arrive at one of the most significant crossroads in the life of their family. But God does not leave Sarai and her family at a crossroads for long. After Terah's death, God calls upon Abram to move to a new land. With this new move comes a new vision for the future. In this case, the couple walks by faith rather than giving into fear of the difficult and unknown path ahead.

EMBRACING THE TRUTH
10-15 Minutes

LEADER: *This section focuses on helping group members integrate what they've learned from the Bible into their own hearts and lives. Invite volunteers to read the Bible passages.*

Many of us, like Sarai, have found ourselves standing at the crossroads between fear and faith. God is calling us to a new way of life, a new identity, and a new challenge. We often desperately desire God's guidance, while at the same time refusing to give God control over our futures. The end result is a nagging sense of fear, confusion, and, ultimately, regret as we look back over our lives and realize that we have literally fought against God's ways.

1. Contrast our common attitude with that of the "noble wife" described in Proverbs 31. Verse 25 is an especially vivid description of a faith-filled woman: *"She is clothed with strength and dignity, and she laughs without fear of the future"* (NLT).

The gnawing anxiety that so often overshadows our journey of faith does not come from God. The desperate need to control our destinies comes from within. We would love to be women who live with strength and dignity, laughing without fear at the days to come.

God has not given us a spirit of fearfulness, but one of power, love, and sound judgment.

2 TIMOTHY 1:7, HCSB

³ Trust in the LORD and do what is good; dwell in the land and live securely. ⁴ Take delight in the LORD, and He will give you your heart's desires. ⁵ Commit your way to the LORD; trust in Him, and He will act, ⁶ making your righteousness shine like the dawn, your justice like the noonday. ⁷ Be silent before the LORD and wait expectantly for Him.

PSALM 37:3-7a, HCSB

2. How has fearfulness at times interfered with your ability to live with "power, love, and sound judgment"?

3. According Psalm 37:3-7, how does God respond to us when we take our fears to Him? From what fears do you need God to deliver you?

4. What in your life needs to change so you will make the time to be silent before God and wait expectantly for Him? What attitudes do you need to change so you can wait without complaining, fear, cynicism, or despair?

CONNECTING *-10-15 Minutes*

LEADER: Use "Connecting" as a time to begin to bond with, encourage, and support one another. Invite everyone to join in the discussions. Provide a kaleidoscope. Pass it around, encouraging each participant to enjoy its many images as you discuss the following questions.

FRAGMENTED VISION

A kaleidoscope is a beautiful thing, especially when you consider that its many wonderful images are made by loose pieces of colored glass and mirrors. The colored glass pieces tumble around in a seemingly random manner, creating the beautiful images we see. Multiple small mirrors and lenses inside the kaleidoscope contribute to the picture, making an orderly pattern out of what would appear to be random pieces.

We are much like Sarah, who had a fragmented vision of God's glorious future plans for her. Because she didn't fully trust God and apply His promises in her life, she struggled under her own power and made many tragic mistakes—mistakes that would drastically affect her family.

1. Have you ever looked at the many facets of your life and seen only randomness? Describe a recent time of barrenness when you couldn't make sense of your past, didn't know where God was leading, or worried that you might not be up to His challenges.

2. Why do you think we so often define ourselves by our barrenness— those areas where we come up short?

Session One

3. How do the people around you try to cope with their emptiness? How do you tend to cope with yours?

4. What do you believe God might be trying to accomplish through your emptiness? How would your life be different if you allowed God to fill your empty places?

5. How do you discern God's will for you in crossroads times? Where do you find support, wisdom, and comfort in your crossroads times?

Principle for Living

God's followers continually face the challenge of living in fear or living in faith. Your response in these times is the clearest indicator of what you truly believe in your innermost being about God's character.

LEADER: Take some extra time to go over the Group Covenant at the back of the book (page 97). Now is the time for each person to pass around her book to collect contact information on the Group Directory on page 104.

Share and record group prayer requests that you will regularly pray over between now and next session. In addition, pray together that God will strengthen and encourage each participant as she takes her heart's questions to God this week. How can the members of this group pray for you?

PRAYER REQUESTS:

TAKING IT HOME

Studying God's truth is not an end in itself. Our goal is always heart and life change. To take the next step of integrating the truth into our lives, we need to (1) look honestly into our hearts to understand the true motivations that drive us, and (2) seek God's perspective on our lives. Psalm 51:6, NASB says God "desire[s] truth in the innermost being."

QUESTIONS TO TAKE TO MY HEART

The following question asks you to look into your heart and focus on your deepest feelings about yourself. Our behaviors are the best indicators of what we really believe deep down. Look deep into the underlying beliefs in your heart where your truest attitudes and motivations live. Spend some time reflecting, and don't settle for a quick answer.

❧ *What does my fear of the future reveal about my relationship with God? In what areas of my life am I failing to apply God's promises?*

❧ *What big decisions am I facing? How will I make these decisions from a core of faith, not fear?*

Session One

A QUESTION TO TAKE TO GOD

When you ask God a question, expect His Spirit to guide your heart to discover His truth. Be careful not to rush or manufacture an answer. Don't write down what you think the "right answer" is. Don't turn the Bible into a reference book or spiritual encyclopedia. Just pose a question to God and wait on Him. Remember, the litmus test for anything we hear from God is alignment with the Bible as our ultimate source of truth. Keep a journal of the insights you gain from your time with God.

  ❧ *Lord, how is my fear keeping me from sincerely loving and serving You? What barriers or false beliefs prevent me from turning over full control of my life and my emotions to You, so that I may honor you with faithful and cheerful obedience?*

Scripture Notes

GENESIS 11:27-31; 12:1-9

11:26 Abram, Nahor and Haran. Haran was the father of Lot, one of the main characters in the story of Sodom and Gomorrah's destruction. The Bible records the fact that Haran, Lot's father, died. According to custom, Abram became responsible for his nephew.

11:28 Ur of the Chaldeans. The starting point for Sarai and her extended family was either (1) the famous Ur in modern Iraq or (2) Ur in Anatolia or modern Syria/Turkey. Since Abram's servant, and later Jacob, went to Paddan Aram to their kinfolk (Gen. 25:20; 28:2), the second Ur in the north might be correct. If it's the first option of the ancient city of Ur, now in modern Iraq, is described by archeologists and biblical scholars believed it was a "flourishing and prosperous society" located along a prominent trade route.

11:30 barren. Sarai was unable to have children. This foreshadows God's provision. God would soon promise to make Abram the father of many nations by miraculously giving his barren wife a child.

11:31 Haran. This city played an important role in Abram's family. It became Abram's first home on his way to Canaan. Generations later, his descendants Isaac and Jacob would find their wives in Haran.

12:1 Go out from your land. Before there was a promising future, Abram needed to renounce his past. He had to leave the familiar in order to find his future. Abram left Ur to head to Haran. And from Haran, he eventually settled in Canaan.

12:2-3 I will bless you. God did not predict Abram's future. He promised it. His promise to Abram assured him of a land, a nation, and a blessing. At 75 years of age, who would not long to receive such a promise? However, at that time, Abram could not have imagined the extent of God's promise. Out of his descendants the entire Jewish nation, the land of Israel, and, eventually, the Savior Himself would arise.

12:4 Abram went. Delay was not in Abram's vocabulary. Although he was short on specific instructions, Abram packed up his belongings, gathered his nephew Lot, and got going. Despite his shortcomings, Abram's life is often a model of faith in action.

12:5 people he had acquired. Abram's response to God's promise affected several people in the immediate picture. Of course, his family members were included. But his extended "family" of servants and workers who tended his wealth of flocks and herds were also affected by the news.

12:7 The LORD appeared. While the Lord's appearance would be an unusual event to most modern readers, it was not an uncommon experience for Abram. The altar became a special symbol between God and Abram. When God appeared to Abram and affirmed His promise to him, Abram often built an altar to remember the experience. The stone and earthen altar would remain as a visible reminder of his journey of faith.

12:8 Bethel. About 12 miles north of Jerusalem is Bethel, a landmark in Jewish history. The site of another of Abram's altars, the city of Bethel also marked the future place of Jacob's dream and housed the Ark of the Covenant for some time as well.

12:9 Negev. Abram's route took him through the Negev, literally "dry land"—referring to the southern desert wasteland. At the end of this desert trip, Abram would be eager for the resources found in the lush landscape of nearby Egypt.

JEREMIAH 2:13

2:13 cracked cisterns. Note the contrast between God and the pagan deities represented by idols. God was the source of life-sustaining water while the cisterns could not hold even a drop for the people to drink.

2 TIMOTHY 1:7

1:7 spirit of fearfulness. Paul makes this sort of appeal because Timothy is not a forceful person (1 Tim. 4:12).
Power, love, and sound judgment. The resources the Spirit gave Timothy leads not to fearfulness, but to these positive characteristics. All Christians have been given this same spirit of power, love, and sound judgment.

SESSION QUOTATIONS

1 Marc Gafni, *The Mystery of Love* (New York: Atria Books, 2003), p. 25.

2 John MacArthur, *Twelve Extraordinary Women* (Nashville: Nelson Books, 2005), p. 34.

DÉJÀ VU ALL OVER AGAIN

As we began our study, we met Sarai at the crossroads of fear and faith. Sarai, whom God renamed Sarah (Genesis 17:5), and her husband Abram (renamed Abraham in Genesis 17:5) had just received an amazing promise from God. Because they trusted Him, they uprooted their household and followed God's leading to a new land. When they reached their destination, Abraham expressed his faithfulness and gratitude to God by building an altar. Surely as he and Sarai paused to worship, the couple's hearts were bursting with hope and confidence.

Soon, however, Abraham and Sarah would find themselves on a spiritual journey common to all of us: they allowed circumstances to unsettle their faith, and their trust in God faltered. One moment, they were affirming the promises of God. The next, they were devising their own schemes for self-protection that were outside God's plans for them. Abraham and Sarah fell into old ruts and patterns of behavior that would leave painful consequences.

BREAKING THE ICE - *15-20 Minutes*

LEADER INSTRUCTIONS FOR THE GROUP EXPERIENCE:
These "Breaking the Ice" experiences are designed to get people talking, but be sure to keep things moving. Before the meeting begins, set up a DVD player. Be sure to bring a DVD of the film, Groundhog Day, *which stars Bill Murray and Andie MacDowell. Read the following "Stuck in a Rut" introduction and then show the second half of Scene 21 "Phil kidnaps Phil" into the beginning of Scene 22 (start at 1:02:50 and watch to around 1:06:33 on the DVD timer). After viewing the scene together, discuss the following questions.*

STUCK IN A RUT

In the movie *Groundhog Day*, Bill Murray plays weatherman Phil Connors, a self-centered, egotistical pessimist. He finds himself stuck in an endless time loop on Groundhog Day in Punxsutawney, Pennsylvania. Each morning at 6:00 A.M., he awakes and faces the same day over and over. If he does nothing different, events repeat as on the original day. But if he changes his behavior, people respond to his new actions, opening up all kinds of possibilities for directing the outcome of events. In the scene that follows, he has given up in despair.

1. Describe a personal "déjà vu" moment.

2. In the film, to what did Phil resort when he'd given up hope of breaking out of his rut through his own schemes and manipulation? Why do you think that strategy was also ineffective?

3. Do you recall how many times Phil tried to do himself in before he realized that this too was useless? Why do you think people tend to do the same things over and over expecting different results?

LEADER: Encourage group members to share insight from the "Taking It Home" questions. This should only take a couple of minutes, but allow more time if someone has a unique insight or needs the support of the group.

4. What did you learn in your "Taking It Home" time this past week? What did God say to you about your fears and your need to turn over your future to Him?

DISCOVERING THE TRUTH
25-30 Minutes

LEADER: For "Discovering the Truth," ask various group members to read sections of the Bible passages aloud. Be sure to leave time for the "Embracing the Truth" and "Connecting" segments that follow.

OLD HABITS DIE HARD

Just as Sarah, and later Hagar, seemed to always be on a journey to someplace new, we all travel faith journeys that lead us to new places along unfamiliar and difficult paths. One moment we're affirming God's goodness in our lives and committing ourselves to following His will.

The next moment, we're knotted with anxiety and falling into old patterns of self-serving and destructive attitudes and actions.

[10] *There was a famine in the land, so Abraham went down to Egypt to live there for a while because the famine in the land was severe.* [11] *When he was about to enter Egypt, he said to his wife Sarah, "Look, I know what a beautiful woman you are.* [12] *When the Egyptians see you, they will say, 'This is his wife.' They will kill me but let you live.* [13] *Please say you're my sister so it will go well for me because of you, and my life will be spared on your account."*

[14] *When Abraham entered Egypt, the Egyptians saw that the woman was very beautiful.* [15] *Pharaoh's officials saw her and praised her to Pharaoh, so the woman was taken to Pharaoh's house.* [16] *He treated Abraham well because of her, and Abraham acquired flocks and herds, male and female donkeys, male and female slaves, and camels.* [17] *But the LORD struck Pharaoh and his house with severe plagues because of Abraham's wife Sarah.* [18] *So Pharaoh sent for Abraham and said, "What have you done to me? Why didn't you tell me she was your wife?* [19] *Why did you say, 'She's my sister,' so that I took her as my wife? Now, here's your wife. Take her and go!"* [20] *Then Pharaoh gave his* *men orders about him, and they sent him away, with his wife and all he had.*

GENESIS 12:10-20, HCSB

Not long after receiving God's promise of blessing on their bloodline, Abraham and Sarah made a choice in direct conflict with God's plan. Abraham realized it was a common practice in Egypt for the king to take into his harem any unmarried woman he liked. The only way to justify taking a married woman was to ensure her husband was dead. As we mentioned in Session One, there is some truth to Abraham's scheme. Sarah was Abraham's half-sister, but there is no such thing as a half-lie.

LEADER: Discuss as many discovery questions as time permits. Encourage participation by inviting different individuals to respond. It will help to highlight in advance the questions you don't want to miss. Be familiar with the Scripture Notes at the end of this session.

1. What motivated Abraham and Sarah to leave Canaan and move to Egypt? In what ways was the impetus for this journey different than the impetus for the journey from Ur to Canaan (Session One)?

2. Not a single mention is made of Abraham and Sarah seeking God's direction, building an altar to God, or worshiping in relation to this journey. What does this imply to you about their characters and the ruts into which they got stuck?

3. How did Abraham "profit" from his sin of lying and deception? What is your reaction when sin results in prosperity?

4. How did Pharaoh's house suffer for Abraham's and Sarah's decision to live outside the healthy boundaries God had set? How can our independence from God infect others or create negative consequences for innocent people?

It's interesting that God did not call Abraham and Sarah to go to Egypt. Their fear of famine motivated them to travel to Egypt. It's also important to notice that unlike his previous journeys, Abraham did not build an altar in Egypt, and he did not take the time to worship God. In fact, "there is no mention of (Abraham) seeking God again until he comes back to the altar he had built between Bethel and Ai." (Genesis 13:4) [1] The couple chosen by God to create a great nation seemed unable to trust God fully in a strange land.

5. How does a "dry spell" in our times of worship correlate to our tendency to fall into old habit patterns and false beliefs?

Principle for Living

Every sin begins with a lie you accept about God, yourself, others, or the world around you. As you allow your heart desires and beliefs to become distorted, you'll normally experience fear, mistrust of God, and rebellion. To walk faithfully with God, commit to staying deeply connected to Him — the Truth and the Light.

DÉJÀ VU

Abraham and Sarah saw the pain their sin brought upon Pharaoh's household. They also saw God's merciful protection in spite of their selfish, fear-based decisions. You would think Abraham and Sarah would have learned a valuable lesson from their time in Egypt, but the couple was much like us. Deceiving themselves into believing their actions were justifiable, they soon fell again.

LEADER: Invite group members to read the parts of the Narrator, Abraham, Abimelech, and God.

[Narrator] *¹ From there Abraham traveled to the region of the Negev and settled between Kadesh and Shur. While he lived in Gerar, ² Abraham said about his wife Sarah,*

[Abraham] *"She is my sister."*

[Narrator] *So Abimelech king of Gerar had Sarah brought to him. ³ But God came to Abimelech in a dream by night and said to him,*

[God] *"You are about to die because of the woman you have taken, for she is a married woman."*

[Narrator] *⁴ Now Abimelech had not approached her, so he said,*

[Abimelech] *"Lord, would you destroy a nation even though it is innocent? ⁵ Didn't he himself say to me, 'She is my sister'? And she herself said, 'He is my brother.' I did this with a clear conscience and clean hands."*

[Narrator] *⁶ Then God said to him in the dream,*

[God] *"Yes, I know that you did this with a clear conscience. I have also kept you from sinning against Me. Therefore I have not let you touch her. ⁷ Now return the man's wife, for he is a prophet, and he will pray for you and you will live. But if you do not return her, know that you will certainly die, you and all who are yours."*

[Narrator] *⁸ Early in the morning Abimelech got up, called all his servants together, and personally told them all these things; and the men were terrified. ⁹ Then Abimelech called Abraham in and said to him,*

[Abimelech] *"What have you done to us? How did I sin against you that you have brought such enormous guilt on me and on my kingdom? You have done things to me that should never be done." ¹⁰ ... "What did you intend when you did this thing?"*

[Abraham] *¹¹ "I thought, 'There is absolutely no fear of God in this place. They will kill me because of my wife.' ¹² Besides, she really is my sister, the daughter of my father though not the daughter of my mother, and she became my wife. ¹³ So when God had me wander from my father's house, I said to her: Show your loyalty to me wherever we go, and say about me: 'He's my brother.'"*

[Narrator] *¹⁴ Then Abimelech took sheep and cattle and male and female slaves, gave them to Abraham, and returned his wife Sarah to him. ¹⁵ Abimelech said,*

[Abimelech] *"Look, my land is before you. Settle wherever you want."* ¹⁶ *And to Sarah he said, "Look, I am giving your brother 1,000 pieces of silver. It is a verification of your honor to all who are with you. You are fully vindicated."*

[Narrator] ¹⁷ *Then Abraham prayed to God, and God healed Abimelech, his wife, and his female slaves so that they could bear children,* ¹⁸ *for the LORD had completely closed all the wombs in Abimelech's household on account of Sarah, Abraham's wife.*

GENESIS 20:1-18, HCSB

6. What does God's communication with Abimelech (verses 3-7) reveal about Abimelech's character and relationship with God?

7. Contrast Abimelech's answer to God in verse 5 with Abraham's answer to Abimelech in verses 11-13. Where did each of them place the blame? Who demonstrated the deeper spiritual discernment and a fear of God in this situation? Explain.

8. How did God demonstrate mercy to Abimelech, Abraham, and Sarah? Why do you think God protected Abraham and Sarah from suffering the consequences of their poor choices and sins?

When Abraham and Sarah first tried this scheme of lying to protect themselves in Egypt, they were 75 and 65 years old, respectively. On their journey through Gerar they were 99 and 89. Over the years, they had seen God provide for them and renew His promise to them. They had been reassured of God's goodness many times.

9. What do you think caused the couple to fall back into this old habit pattern? How can our environments and the people closest to us encourage us to slide back into destructive ruts of behavior and attitude?

Principle for Living

No matter how strong your personal relationship with God, you must be spiritually alert to avoid sliding back into old patterns of false beliefs, distorted thinking, and behaviors not aligned with God's plan for you.

EMBRACING THE TRUTH
15-20 Minutes

LEADER: This section focuses on helping group members integrate what they've learned from the Bible into their own hearts and lives. Invite volunteers to read the Bible passages aloud.

It's easy to wonder why Abraham and Sarah can't just break out of an old destructive cycle. Given God's promises to them, it seems it shouldn't be difficult to discern or at least to trust in God's will.

1. What are some lies people tell themselves in order to justify their sins or destructive behaviors? What distorted desires and/or false beliefs about God do you think might drive these attitudes and behaviors?

2. How can regret over past sins and failures keep us from pursuing God-centered lives today?

No human is perfect, and the temptation to fall back into sinful patterns of self-reliance is always there. That's why first Corinthians 10:12 warns, "Therefore, whoever thinks he stands must be careful not to fall" (HCSB).

3. How can we take care to guard against temptation's slippery slope and the lures that draw us back into a self-defeating lifestyle?

God is merciful *and* redemptive — He longs to forgive our sins and restore us to His path. Even in His amazing compassion, God will never force His ways on us though. It's up to us to turn back — to realign our priorities, choices, and decisions with His ways. Read parts of Psalm 51, written by a man who failed greatly, and yet was called "a man after God's own heart."

[A Psalm of David, when Nathan the prophet came to him, after he had slept with Bathsheba and killed her husband.]
¹ Be gracious to me, O God, according to Your lovingkindness; according to the greatness of Your compassion blot out my transgressions. ² Wash me thoroughly from my iniquity and cleanse me from my sin. ... ⁴ Against You, You only, I have sinned and done what is evil in Your sight, so that You are justified when You speak and blameless when You judge. ...
⁶ Behold, You desire truth in the innermost being, and in the hidden part You will make me know wisdom. ...
¹² Restore to me the joy of Your salvation and sustain me with a willing spirit. ¹³ Then I will teach transgressors Your ways, and sinners will be converted to You.

PSALM 51:1-2,4,6,12-13, NASB

4. How should seeing God's mercy towards Abraham and Sarah, as well as David, affect your willingness to turn from your failures and to seek God's restoration?

5. What key elements in Psalm 51 strike you about confession (verses 1-4), repentance or change (verse 6), and restoration (verses 12-13)?

It's only through a continual attitude of humility and dependence that we will choose to trust God rather than relying on ourselves. A continual attitude of repentance does not make us weak; rather, it enables us to keep rekindling our belief in God's goodness and power. Often, like Sarah, we turn to God only when our own resources lead us into trouble.

Principle for Living

True repentance involves a change in what you believe in your "innermost being" about God and His will for your life. Your journey begins when you honestly admit the condition of your life, rather than denying the truth or blaming others. God will use your grief to restore you!

CONNECTING *- 5-10 Minutes*

Session Two

LEADER INSTRUCTIONS FOR THE GROUP EXPERIENCE:
Use "Connecting" as a time to develop closeness within your group. Encourage and support one another as you invite group members to be open in sharing a part of their lives with each other. For the group experience, give each person a few strips of construction paper, some tape, and a marker. Place a trash can in the middle of the group circle.

REDEEMING REGRETS

When you're nearing the end of life, will you praise God for His blessings and guidance along your faith journey, or will you grit your teeth in regret over foolish decisions, misguided mistakes, and missed opportunities for blessing? Every day of your life is a new day to repent of the past, erase the regret, and re-commit to God's path. As Sarah found, you'll discover that God longs to restore you.

ACTIVITY: (1) On each strip of paper handed out by your leader, write a déjà vu issue or sin (in action or attitude) with which you struggle. (2) After writing on a few strips of paper, loop and tape the strips together into a paper chain. (3) Then, take time in silent prayer to repent of each of these sins and ask for God's forgiveness and wisdom. Each time you pray over a link, break that link and throw it in the trash. (4) When everyone is finished with their chains, discuss how you felt during this activity.

The story of Sarah and Abraham shows us that God can redeem our regrets. He'll pick up the pieces of our poor choices and faithless wanderings, bringing us back into His "good, pleasing, and perfect will" (Romans 12:2). As we persevere on the journey with Him through life's ups and downs, He will give us the resources to leave behind old patterns and attitudes. He continually woos us into deeper intimacy and determined trust in Him.

Share and record group prayer requests that you will regularly pray over between now and the next session. Also pray together today, asking God to help each one to find healing and restoration through turning to God for truth rather than relying on herself.

PRAYER REQUESTS:

TAKING IT HOME

Studying God's truth is not an end in itself. Our goal is always heart and life change. To take the next step of integrating the truth into our lives, we need to (1) look honestly into our hearts to understand the true motivations that drive us, and (2) seek God's perspective on our lives. Psalm 51:6, NASB says God "desire[s] truth in the innermost being."

A QUESTION TO TAKE TO MY HEART

The following question asks you to look into your heart and focus on your deepest feelings about yourself. Our behaviors are the best indicators of what we really believe deep down. We should especially seek to understand our déjà vu issues. Look deep into the underlying beliefs in your heart where your truest attitudes and motivations live.

Read all of Psalm 51 and reflect on the condition of your own heart as you read the outpourings from David's heart. Then ask yourself this question:

❧ What are my key déjà vu issues? What lies do I believe about God or myself that are leading me away from God's best for my life?

Session Two

A QUESTION TO TAKE TO GOD

When you ask God a question, expect His Spirit to guide your heart to discover His truth. Be careful not to rush or manufacture an answer. Don't write down what you think the "right answer" is. Don't turn the Bible into a reference book or spiritual encyclopedia. Before you turn to your Bible, just pose a question to God and wait on Him. Remember, the litmus test for anything we hear from God is alignment with the Bible as our ultimate source of truth. Keep a journal of the insights you gain from your times with God.

❧ *Lord, how do You feel about my déjà vu issues? What false beliefs or distorted desires are at the root of theses ruts in my life?*

SCRIPTURE NOTES

GENESIS 12:10-20; 20:1-17

12:10 went down to Egypt. How easy it would have been for Abram to give up on God's promises at the point of the famine? Instead of giving up, Abram was going on to Egypt, where the Nile River provided year-round resources.

12:11 beautiful. Many admired Sarai because of her beauty. Abram feared her beauty would impede their safe travel among potentially desirous male suitors.

12:13 say you're my sister. Abram tried to rationalize his lie since Sarai was, in fact, his half-sister. However, his lie was a losing proposition for all involved. If Pharaoh had believed this lie, Sarai could have been permanently added to his harem. If Pharaoh knew the truth that Sarai was married to Abram, he would have had to kill Abram to receive her.

12:16 He treated Abram well because of her. As a gesture of kindness, Pharaoh rewarded Abram with livestock, camels, and other farm animals. Abram added these to his already large array of animals. Cattle and servants were an ancient measure of wealth; this deal between the pharaoh and Abraham must have increased Abraham's wealth significantly.

12:19 Why did you say ... sister? Caught in a lie, Abram faced the Pharaoh's caustic anger and quickly excused himself from the Pharaoh's presence. Even in light of God's infinite resources, Abram's reliance upon his own resources and cleverness was a lesson he would too soon repeat.

20:2 Abimelech. As with many Old Testament names, this king had a son or grandson by the same name in (26:1).

20:3 dream. Dreams were one of the more common ways God got the attention of people in these days. He used this nocturnal opportunity to offer caution or provide guidance. In this case, God uses a dream to orchestrate circumstances so that Sarah will be able to bear the child he promised Abraham.

20:11 fear of God. What Abraham means is that this community had no indicators that God was known or revered. When the phrase "fear of God" is used in Scripture, it does not suggest fright or fearful apprehension, but rather worshipful respect and allegiance.

20:12 she really is my sister. Even though Abraham was half right, his deception was completely wrong as far as God was concerned. Attempting to shade the truth to save our lives is an affront to God's promise to save us even when there's no obvious escape.

20:16 pieces of silver. The king felt obligated to compensate Abraham for the inconvenience he had caused. The pieces of silver were measured by weight in shekels. Shekels were the most common currency in this period.

PSALM 51:1-6

51:1-2 Be gracious. While the context belonged to David, this prayer models a universal need for mercy.

51:4 Against You, You only, I have sinned. David wrote this psalm in response to Nathan's rebuke for his adultery with Bathsheba. David recognizes that his sin is a violation first against God and then against Uriah.

51:6 truth in the innermost being. David—he who loves God's ways—is overwhelmed by how willfully he has sinned. David realizes that he cannot keep God's laws without God's help, and he prays that God will create truth in him that will transcend his sinful patterns of belief and behavior.

SESSION QUOTATIONS

1 Wayne Barber, Eddie Rasnake, and Richard Shepherd, *Life Principles from the Old Testament* (Chattanooga: AMG Publishers, 1999), p. 49.

Session Two

LARGE AND IN CHARGE

In Session Two, we watched Sarah and Abraham slip back into some well-worn ruts of thinking and behavior that ran in a different direction than God's best paths. Fortunately, God is full of mercy and came to their rescue.

For 10 long years, Abraham and Sarah continue to wonder daily if *this* will be the day when God fulfills His promise. But God is silent, and Sarah's womb remains empty. As the days stretch into months and the months into years, the couple begins to question whether they understood God correctly.

BREAKING THE ICE - *15-20 Minutes*

LEADER INSTRUCTIONS FOR THE GROUP EXPERIENCE:
A brief movie clip will open discussions on today's topic. Be sure to bring a DVD of **Forrest Gump**, *which stars Tom Hanks and Sally Field. Set up a DVD player before the meeting begins. Read the following introduction and then show Scene 14, "Mama's Trip to Heaven," (on the DVD timer from 1:38:47 to about 1:43:00 where he says he cuts the grass free). Discuss the questions that follow.*

LIFE'S A BOX OF CHOCOLATES

In the movie *Forrest Gump*, Tom Hanks plays a man from the rural South with a minor mental handicap. Hanks explains that Forrest believes in three things — God, his mama, and his friend Jenny — filtering everything else through those three grids. He's a very simple person who does extraordinary things. In his innocence, amazing things seemingly happen by accident.

1. What do you think about the "box of chocolates" philosophy?

2. Explain what it means to "make your own destiny." Is this form of taking charge positive or a negative? Explain your thoughts.

3. Do you think it's possible to balance taking charge of your own destiny with following God's will for your life? Explain or give an example.

LEADER: Encourage group members to share insight from the "Taking It Home" questions. This should only take a couple of minutes, but allow more time if someone has a unique insight or needs the support of the group.

4. In your "Taking It Home" assignment, what insights did you gain into your déjà vu issues? Did God reveal any false beliefs or distorted desires at the root of the well-worn patterns of thinking or behavior into which you keep sliding?

DISCOVERING THE TRUTH
20-25 Minutes

LEADER: For "Discovering the Truth," ask various group members to read the Bible passages aloud. Be sure to leave time for the "Embracing the Truth" and "Connecting" segments that follow this discussion.

IT'S UP TO ME

[1] *Abram's wife Sarai had not borne him children. She owned an Egyptian slave named Hagar.* [2] *Sarai said to Abram, "Since the LORD has prevented me from bearing children, go to my slave; perhaps I can have children by her." And Abram agreed to what Sarai said.* [3] *So Abram's wife Sarai took Hagar, her Egyptian slave, and gave her to her husband Abram as a wife for him. This happened after Abram had lived in the land of Canaan 10 years.*

[4] *He slept with Hagar, and she became pregnant. When she realized that she was pregnant, she looked down on her mistress.* [5] *Then Sarai said to Abraham, "You are responsible for my suffering! I put my slave in your arms, and ever since she saw that she was pregnant, she has looked down on me. May the LORD judge between me and you."* [6] *Abram replied to Sarai, "Here, your slave is in your hands; do whatever you want with her." Then Sarai mistreated her so much that she ran away from her.*

GENESIS 12:10-20, HCSB

Session Three

1. To what does Sarah attribute her barrenness (verse 2)? Why do you think we find it difficult to wait on God's timing and methods?

Sarah had never heard directly from God about her part in the promise to Abraham; she could only hope. After 10 years of uncertainty, she grew especially impatient. Sara decided to take matters into her own hands, effectively tying knots into the family fabric that God alone could untangle.

2. What part of Abraham and Sarah's issues also became Hagar's (verses 4 and 6)? How do you feel about what happened to Hagar in this story?

Although the situation in Genesis 16 sounds strange—even immoral— it's understandable given the cultural practices of the time. Archeologists have discovered marriage contracts on tablets, which specify that a wife, if she cannot bear children, has the responsibility to provide a woman for her husband to supply an heir. Cultural practices, however, in no way excuse rushing ahead of God's direction or doing things our way instead of His.

3. In what ways could Hagar's pregnancy and her son's legal position as Abraham's and Sarah's firstborn heir have created a source of tension and conflict between the women?

It's important to realize that according to ancient law, any child born of a slave and a free man became the responsibility of the wife of the free man. Hagar's son would legally be considered Sarah's child, and was liable to inherit all of Abraham's wealth. If the boy had retained his status as the firstborn child, he might have contested with any of Sarah's biological offspring to receive their father's blessing, authority in the family, and possessions after his death.

Session Three

In our culture, people who take charge and make things happen are often rewarded. Sarah thought she knew best and decided to move ahead without consulting God. She soon realized that her solution was flawed, but the wheels were already set in motion for a major collision.

Principle for Living
When facing difficult circumstances in your walk with God, avoid trying to solve your problems with your own human wisdom apart from God's wisdom. Waiting for something you desire is never easy, but God wants you to trust Him even when it doesn't seem reasonable.

A RESCUER

Hagar was a woman whose dream for family and motherhood didn't go the way she planned—and dreamed about since girlhood. It seems she was forced into a no-win situation. Though it's easy to dismiss Hagar's arrogance as ugly and petty, we should remember that she was given little choice. Sarah, on the other hand, has no excuse for her own harsh treatment of her maidservant. It's not surprising given the circumstances that it was Hagar—not Sarah—who received special divine comfort when the messy family situation worsened.

⁷ The Angel of the LORD found her [Hagar] by a spring of water in the wilderness, the spring on the way to Shur. ⁸ He said, "Hagar, slave of Sarai, where have you come from, and where are you going?" She replied, "I'm running away from my mistress Sarai." ⁹

Then the Angel of the LORD said to her, "You must go back to your mistress and submit to her mistreatment." ¹⁰ The Angel of the LORD also said to her, "I will greatly multiply your offspring, and they will be too many to count." ¹¹ Then the Angel of the LORD said to her: You have conceived and will have a son. You will name him Ishmael, for the LORD has heard your cry of affliction. ¹² This man will be like a wild donkey. His hand will be against everyone, and everyone's hand will be against him; he will live at odds with all his brothers.

¹³ So she named the LORD who spoke to her: The God Who Sees, for she said, "Have I really seen here the One who sees me?" ¹⁴ That is why she named the spring, "A Well of the Living One Who Sees Me." It is located between Kadesh and Bered. ¹⁵ So Hagar gave birth to Abram's son, and Abram gave the name Ishmael to the son Hagar had. ¹⁶ Abram was 86 years old when Hagar bore Ishmael to him.

GENESIS 16:7-16, HCSB

4. Hagar ran away in panic from her life (verse 6). How must Hagar have felt about her circumstances, herself, and those she thought she could trust? What kind of life could she expect with the problems she had and the choices she'd made?

5. Assuming that this angel is aware of divine knowledge or is actually God Himself, what purpose might be behind the question the angel asked Hagar in verse 8?

6. How is the promise given to Hagar in verses 10-12 similar to and different from the promise given to Abraham and Sarah in Genesis 12 (Session 1)?

7. It's common in the Bible for people to give God a new name when they discover a new, exciting characteristic about Him. Given the way Hagar named God and the place where He met her, what new truths do you think Hagar learned about God and the way He related to her personally?

Alone in the desert and feeling completely alone, Hagar knew where she had come from, but she had no clue where she was going. That's what made the angel's question about her past circumstances and future so poignant (verse 8). The angel forced Hagar to feel her own weakness, lack of wisdom, and powerlessness. In doing this, he opened her mind to the fact that God alone was in control.

The amazing news is that God longs to come to us and rescue us. When God found Hagar in the wilderness, feeling abandoned and hopeless, she was embracing her pain rather than trying to cover it up or ignore it. Though she was a slave, a woman, and a nobody in the eyes of her culture—God *knew* all about her. ***He heard her heart's cry!*** She was overwhelmed that God saw her, felt her pain, and cared deeply about her.

Principle for Living
Sometimes God allows you to feel your own weakness so that you'll realize your need for His intervention and cry out to Him. Rather than killing your heart, God wants you to embrace your pain, knowing that He's "the Living One Who Sees" you!

The angel gave Hagar a glorious promise, that she would bear a son and have a lasting legacy through her numerous descendants. Her son, whom she would name Ishmael, would be a nomad. He would experience great strife with his neighbors, but he would father a great nation—just as his future half-brother would do. Ishmael was included as a part of God's promise to Abraham and Sarah. Surely when she presented him to Abraham, Hagar assumed her part in the family story was complete. But time would reveal that the birth of Ishmael would hardly solve the family's problems. In fact, it would only create new challenges—just as best laid plans often do when we move ahead without God.

EMBRACING THE TRUTH
15-20 Minutes

LEADER: This section focuses on helping group members integrate what they've learned from the Bible story into their own hearts and lives. Invite volunteers to read the Bible passages aloud.

THE ANXIETY TRAP

In their book *Life Principles from the Old Testament,* the authors write, "Trusting God is not characterized by anxiety. Anxiety is a warning sign that you are depending on yourself or circumstances rather than God to accomplish His purpose." [1] How well this statement summarizes Sarah's problem, while pointing a finger at an issue with which we all struggle. We can easily allow stress and anxiety to take God's rightful place in our lives, letting it govern how we think and what we do.

1. What cultural values can interfere with our commitment to following God? What stressors crowd their way into our hearts?

2. Share a "waiting time" or anxious time in your own life. What questions did you ask yourself? What questions did you ask God? What fears or anxieties surfaced?

A HEART SHIELD

God instructs us in Proverbs 4:23: *"Above all else, guard your heart, for it is the wellspring of life"* (NIV). That's the reason Paul encouraged the struggling Philippians with words about anxiety, and Proverbs discusses trust.

⁶ Don't worry about anything, but in everything, through prayer and petition with thanksgiving, let your requests be made known to God. ⁷ And the peace of God, which surpasses every thought, will guard your hearts and your minds in Christ Jesus.

PHILIPPIANS 4:6-7, HCSB

Trust in the LORD with all your heart; do not depend on your own understanding. Seek his will in all you do, and he will direct your paths.

PROVERBS 3:5-6, NLT

3. According to Philippians 4 and Proverbs 3, how are anxiety and trust in God related? What heart beliefs about God, ourselves, or the world in which we live can drive us away from trusting?

4. In what areas of your life are you regularly experiencing anxiety or stress? How is this anxiety affecting your trust in God?

Session Three

5. Share a time when you have experienced the "peace of God" described in Philippians 4:7 or when you clearly trusted God to direct your path.

Principle for Living

God wants to honor sound thinking and responsible actions. However, you can easily compound your problems and damage your heart when you fail to pray and consult God's Word for divine wisdom and guidance—when you depend on your own understanding or allow anxiety to rule you.

***LEADER INSTRUCTIONS FOR THE GROUP EXPERIENCE:** Prior to meeting, cut shield shapes out of construction paper or card stock; each participant will need one. Also provide colored markers.*

The word for surpasses in Philippians 4:7 literally means "to have authority" or "to govern." The word for guard means, "to shield." So Paul is saying, *"And the peace of God, which has authority over every thought, will shield your heart and mind through Christ Jesus."*

Your leader will pass around paper shields and colored markers. As she does, read and meditate on Philippians 4:6-7. Then, on your shield, write a prayer to God that praises Him for His goodness and guidance and turns over your anxieties to Him.

CONNECTING *- 10-15 Minutes*

*   **LEADER:** Use "Connecting" as a time to encourage one another to draw closer to God. Set the tone for openness and support by sharing first and affirming each group member for sharing with the group.*

OUT OF OUR DESERTS

Sooner or later, we run as Hagar did into our own wilderness of fear, shame, abandonment, anger, or self-protection only to find ourselves just surviving—not really living—in a foreign, desolate land. You may feel like you've been wandering in a desert lately, ever aware of your losses. Or you may have made a futile decision long ago to try to put your desert experience behind you—to bury it and try to disconnect your heart and life from it.

1. Describe a time in your life when you tried to run from a problem or tried to slide out of your situation without anyone noticing. How did it work out?

2. Describe a time when God redeemed your poor choices. What negative side effects of your choices did you experience in spite of the good that God brought about?

God hears your heart's cry! He sees you and feels your pain. He longs for you to look back on this time in your life and ask with Hagar, "Have I truly seen the One who sees me?" Often in our times of disappointment, confusion, and waiting, we just need to know that God has His eyes on us.

3. How might the knowledge that God "sees" you encourage you as you face present or upcoming difficulties?

God is *thrilled* about you, and longs to see you enthused about a freer and deeper life with Him. All too often, we fall into old patterns of thinking and behavior rather than turning to God to meet our deepest needs for intimacy, acceptance, and meaning. God is a relentless lover, but He's also a gentle lover. He wants you to rest in His arms, comforted in those times when you're lost, trapped, or struggling.

4. How does it feel to know that even in the dark places, God is still coming for you? In what area are you waiting for God now?

Share and record group prayer requests that you will regularly pray over between now and next session. Share the anxieties and struggles written on your heart shields and pray together that God will strengthen and encourage each participant, providing His peace to shield her heart and mind in difficulties.

PRAYER REQUESTS:

Taking It Home

LEADER: For this week's "Taking It Home" questions, encourage group members to retreat to a place that's special to each of them for their time with God. Perhaps there's a special mountain, trail, river, garden, or building. For some a bubble bath or sunroom will fit the bill. Encourage each person to set aside quiet time this week so she can make the most of this study and group experience. Remind them to keep a journal of this time.

A Question to Take to My Heart

The following question asks you to look into your heart and focus on your deepest feelings about yourself. Your behavior—not your intellectual stance—is the best indicator of your truest beliefs in your innermost being (Psalm 51:6, NASB). This is spiritual introspection time; look deep into the underlying beliefs in your heart where your truest attitudes and motivations live.

❧ *In what situations am I determined to do life my way instead of God's? What needs or beliefs are really driving this tendency?*

Session Three

43

A QUESTION TO TAKE TO GOD

When you ask God a question, expect His Spirit to guide your heart in His truth. Be careful not to rush or manufacture an answer. Don't write down what you think the "right answer" is. Don't turn the Bible into a reference book or spiritual encyclopedia. Just pose a question to God and wait on Him. Remember, the litmus test for anything we hear form God is alignment with the Bible as our ultimate source of truth. Keep a journal of the insights you gain from your time with God.

    ❦ *God, do You really "see" me? Will You come to my rescue in the way You did for Hagar?*

Scripture Notes

GENESIS 16:1-16

12:10 went down to Egypt. How easy it would have been for Abram to give up on God's promises at the point of the famine. Was this land of shortage the outcome of God's promise? Instead of giving up, Abram was going on to Egypt, where the Nile River provided year-round resources.

16:1 Egyptian slave. More than likely, Abram and Sarai obtained Hagar during their move from Canaan to Egypt with Abram's nephew Lot. Hagar's name means "flight" or "run away."

16:2 prevented me from bearing children. God had not fulfilled His promise (15:4), and Sarai began to doubt. *go to my slave.* The Sumerians had a custom of using a concubine to obtain a male heir in the case of a wife's barrenness. A concubine did not have the same rights as the wife. The man and his wife were legally the child's parents.

16:4 looked down on her mistress. Dissension between Sarai and Hagar was the fruit of Sarai taking matters into her own hands. Childlessness was a great burden to women, for it was seen as a lack of blessing from the Lord. Hagar's pregnancy placed her in a more favored position.

16:5 May the LORD judge. A common statement of doubt or suspicion. The word used for "judge" is Mizpah, which literally means "watchtower."

16:7 The Angel of the LORD. Some think this refers to an appearance of Christ; others say this was a special messenger of God. When God spoke to Abram second time, He was identified as the Angel of the Lord (see Genesis 22:1,15).

16:8 running away ... mistress. Hagar's answer shows her aimlessness. *The Code of Hammurabi* and laws of Mesopotamia prescribed punishments for runaway slaves, some of which were very severe.

16:11 Ishmael. Ishmael's name means "God hears."

16:12 wild ass. A promise of Ishmael's eventual nomadic lifestyle. *live at odds with all his brothers.* Points to the hostility between the descendants of Isaac (the Israelites) and Ishmael (the Ishmaelites).

PHILIPPIANS 4:6-7

4:6 Don't worry. They are to stop being anxious. To worry is to display a lack of confidence in God's care and in God's control over a situation (Matt. 6:25-34). *prayer ... petition ... requests.* Paul uses three synonyms in a row to describe the alternative to anxiety. Instead of worrying, a person ought to converse directly with God and lay out before Him all that is on his or her mind, confident that God will hear and respond.

4:7 the peace of God. This is supernatural peace that comes from God and is focused on Him. *surpasses every thought.* Such peace can never fully be understood by human beings, and it can and should govern every thought. *guard.* This is a military term. It describes a garrison of soldiers, such as those stationed at Philippi, whose job it is to stand watch over the city and protect it. It can also describe the task of shielding us from the enemy.

PROVERBS 3:5-6

3:5 with all your heart. The Bible uses this phrase to express total commitment. The "Shema" in Deuteronomy 6:5 calls us to love God with all our hearts, minds, and souls. Jesus described this as the first and greatest commandment.

3:6 direct your paths. This implies more than guidance. It means God intentionally removes obstacles from our path.

SESSION QUOTATIONS

1 Wayne Barber, Eddie Rasnake, and Richard Shepherd, *Life Principles from the Old Testament* (Chattanooga: AMG Publishers, 1999), p. 52.

GOD COMES THROUGH ... PLUS SOME

In our last session, both Sarah and Hagar allowed anxiety to govern their hearts rather than trusting in God "who really sees" us and our life circumstances. Hagar met God in a life-transforming way when she came to the end of her own resources and, in her desperation, cried out to Him. She was overwhelmed and excited to realize that God sees her, cares deeply, and comes to her rescue.

Sarah continues to live in the tangled web of her own making as she learns the difficult lesson of trusting God even when it doesn't seem reasonable. Her solution brought her more heartache than she ever imagined. In this session we'll marvel at the miraculous events God uses to renew Sarah and finally fulfill His promise after so many years.

BREAKING THE ICE - *10-15 Minutes*

LEADER: If possible, obtain a copy of the song "Secondhand Rose" and play it for the group before your "Breaking the Ice" questions. The questions invite group members to share a small part of their stories and will launch into the day's discussion. Keep this time light-hearted.

Barbara Streisand sang "Secondhand Rose," a hit song about a woman whose father ran a second-hand store and provided her with nothing but hand-me-downs. In the song, Rose feels "abused" because she never has anything of her own: everything first belonged to someone else.

1. What was the best "hand-me-down" you got as a child? What made it acceptable or good?

2. What was the worst "hand-me-down" you received? Describe your feelings and reactions to receiving it.

3. Why are hand-me-downs, in spite of their useful nature, often viewed with negativity?

LEADER: Encourage group members to share insight from the "Taking It Home" questions. This should only take a couple of minutes, but allow more time if someone has a unique insight or needs the support of the group.

4. What did you learn about yourself this week as you reflected on tendencies to take charge rather than waiting on God's timing? What did you hear from God about coming to your rescue?

SECONDHAND BLESSINGS

Sarah could have related to Secondhand Rose. Surely as Sarah watched Ishmael growing and winning his father's affection, it seemed like she'd been left out of God's plan for Abraham's legacy. Culture allowed her to play at being Ishmael's mom, but the boy whose life was intended to bring relief from Sarah's barrenness and uncertainty brought grief instead. While Sarah and Abraham got what they wanted—a son—they did not receive the fullness of the blessing that God had promised. In settling for a secondhand blessing, they stopped expecting that God wanted to delight in giving to them.

DISCOVERING THE TRUTH
25-30 Minutes

LEADER: Invite various group members to read the Bible passages aloud. You group should be gelling well now and enjoying discussions. Be sure to leave time for the "Embracing the Truth" and "Connecting" segments.

HELLO. IS ANYBODY THERE?

For 13 long years after the birth of Ishmael, God remains silent about His promised legacy. During this time, Abraham and Sarah raise Ishmael as their own. There are signs, however, that the tensions and frustrations of this arrangement are wearing. Only time will reveal that the Lord did not forget His promise.

¹ When Abram was 99 years old, the LORD appeared to him, saying, "I am God Almighty. Live in My presence and be devout. ² I will establish My covenant between Me and you, and I will multiply you greatly." ³ Then Abram fell to the ground, and God spoke with him: ⁴ "As for Me, My covenant is with you, and you will become the father of many nations. ⁵ Your name will no longer be Abram, but your name will be Abraham, for I will make you the father of many nations. ⁶ I will make you extremely fruitful and will make nations and kings come from you. ⁷ I will keep My covenant between Me and you, and your offspring after you throughout their generations, as an everlasting covenant to be your God and the God of your offspring after you. ⁸ And to you and your offspring after you I will give the land where you are residing—all the land of Canaan—as an eternal possession, and I will be their God." ⁹ God also said to Abraham, "As for you, you and your offspring after you throughout their generations are to keep My covenant.

GENESIS 17:1-9, HCSB

LEADER: Discuss as many discovery questions as time permits. This section will focus on the fulfillment of God's promise and the couple's reactions. It will help to highlight in advance the questions you don't want to miss. Be familiar with the Scripture Notes at the end of this session.

1. Why do you think God identified Himself as "God Almighty" in this encounter with Abraham more than 20 years after the initial promise? Why is that significant for Abraham and Sarah?

2. In Genesis 12, God promised to make Abraham the father of a great nation. In what ways does this new covenant in Genesis 17 enlarge the earlier promise God gave Abraham and Sarah?

YOU'VE GOT TO BE KIDDING!

¹⁵ God said to Abraham, "As for your wife Sarai, do not call her Sarai, for Sarah will be her name. ¹⁶ I will bless her; indeed, I will give you a son by her. I will bless her, and she will produce nations; kings of peoples will come from her." ¹⁷ Abraham fell to the ground, laughed, and thought in his heart, "Can a child be born to a hundred-year-old man? Can Sarah, a ninety-year-old woman, give birth?" ¹⁸ So Abraham said to God, "If only Ishmael could live in Your presence!" ¹⁹ But God said, "No. Your wife Sarah will bear you a son, and you will name him Isaac. I will confirm My covenant with him as an everlasting covenant for his offspring after him. [20] As for Ishmael, I have heard you. I will certainly bless him; I will make him fruitful and will multiply him greatly. He will father 12 tribal leaders, and I will make him into a great nation. [21] But I will confirm My covenant with Isaac, whom Sarah will bear to you at this time next year."

GENESIS 17:15-21, HCSB

3. Why is it significant that Sarah is mentioned by name in this second promise from God? What promises does God make specifically for her?

4. What change in attitude do you see between the two times that Abraham "fell to the ground" in verses 3 and again in verse 17? What changed?

5. What are some reasons that Abraham might have offered Ishmael as the way that God might fulfill His covenant? What does Abraham's reaction reveal about his beliefs about God? About himself?

6. How does God demonstrate mercy to the whole family in this second promise?

Principle of Living

It's easy to get caught up in life and forget that God is El-Shaddai, God Almighty. You make God too small when you try to limit His infinite wisdom and power. Don't settle for secondhand blessings; joyfully anticipate God's best gifts that will surpass your wildest dreams.

God never altered His original promise to Abraham—He only expanded on it. It seems that Abraham and Sarah had given up on receiving the deepest desires of their hearts, likely even doubting God's heart toward them. Indeed, it appears that the couple had resigned themselves to living with failure and disappointment. How wonderful that God remained constant in spite of their doubts—determined to show them that He honors His promises and loves them even in their failings and the messiness of their lives.

GOD DELIVERS THE MESSAGE TO SARAH

¹ Then the LORD appeared to Abraham at the oaks of Mamre while he was sitting in the entrance of his tent during the heat of the day. ... ⁶ Abraham hurried into the tent and said to Sarah, "Quick! Knead three measures of fine flour and make bread." ⁷ Meanwhile, Abraham ran to the herd and got a tender, choice calf. He gave it to a young man, who hurried to prepare it. ⁸ Then Abraham took curds and milk, and the calf that he had prepared, and set them before the men. He served them as they ate under the tree.

⁹ "Where is your wife Sarah?" they asked him. "There, in the tent," he answered. ¹⁰ The LORD said, "I will certainly come back to you in about a year's time, and your wife Sarah will have a son!" Now Sarah was listening at the entrance of the tent behind him. ¹¹ Abraham and Sarah were old and getting on in years. Sarah had passed the age of childbearing. ¹² So she laughed to herself: "After I have become shriveled up and my lord is old, will I have delight?" ¹³ But the LORD asked Abraham, "Why did Sarah laugh, saying, 'Can I really have a baby when I'm old?' ¹⁴ Is anything impossible for the LORD? At the appointed time I will come back to you, and in about a year she will have a son." ¹⁵ Sarah denied it. "I did not laugh," she said, because she was afraid. But He replied, "No, you did laugh."

GENESIS 18:1,6-15, HCSB

7. This is the third time God has made this promise to Sarah and Abraham. What does Sarah's response in this passage indicate about her view of God? Brainstorm some ways we sometimes display Sarah's attitude.

8. How did God react to Sarah's disbelief? The name God specified for the coming child, Isaac, means "he laughs." What messages do You think God was sending through this name?

Abraham and Sarah actually thought Ishmael was the seed of the promise. They no doubt concluded that God's revelation to Hagar about Ishmael's future sounded just like God's promise to Abraham (compare Genesis 15:5 with 16:10). God's timing often does not make sense to us, but when we take matters into our own hands and try to do things by ourselves, God might allow us to struggle in our own darkness. He wants us to let go of our need for control, our need to understand, and our need to manipulate.

God desires that we constantly seek Him, forever pressing for the blessings He gives to those who love Him.

Principle for Living
As you release your grip on your need to control, to understand, and to manipulate, God will pour out His blessings on you ... in His time and in His way.

EMBRACING THE TRUTH
10-15 Minutes

LEADER: This section focuses on helping group members integrate what they've learned from the Bible into their own hearts and lives. Discussions will highlight topics of God's gifts and our faithfulness. Invite volunteers to read the Bible passages aloud.

THE LAST LAUGH

Abraham and Sarah took desperate measures—like deceiving foreign rulers and forcing Hagar into the role of surrogate mother—to obtain God's blessings. If they had just trusted in God's heart, and in His infinite delight in giving good gifts to His children, they could have waited for God's abundant blessings without strife or anxiety.

[1] The LORD came to Sarah as He had said, and the LORD did for Sarah what He had promised. [2] Sarah became pregnant and bore a son to Abraham in his old age, at the appointed time God had told him. [3] Abraham named his son who was born to him—the one Sarah bore to him—Isaac. [4] When his son Isaac was eight days old, Abraham circumcised him, as God had commanded him. [5] Abraham was 100 years old when his son Isaac was born to him. [6] Sarah said, "God has made me laugh, and everyone who hears will laugh with me." [7] She also said, "Who would have told Abraham that Sarah would nurse children? Yet I have borne him a son in his old age."

GENESIS 21:1-7, HCSB

1. According to verse 2, when did God fulfill His promise to Abraham and Sarah? Share a recent time in your life when you've had trouble waiting for God's "appointed time."

2. Rephrase in your own words what Sarah said in verse 6. How does this laughter compare to the laughter we have seen earlier from Abraham and Sarah?

PURSUING OUR HEART'S DESIRES

3. God's solution for Sarah's barrenness and full healing for her past disappointments was a long time in coming. Was it worth the wait? Why do you suppose that God can take so long, as He did for Sarah, to come to our rescue?

Sometimes in hindsight, we can see why God delayed in responding to a deep need in our lives. At other times we're just unable, from our perspective, to make sense of God's slowness; all we know is that He came at His "appointed time." God's personal visit to Sarah clearly reaffirmed her trust in His goodness and promises. The writer of Hebrews tells us, "By faith even Sarah herself, when she was barren, received power to conceive offspring, even though she was past the age, since she considered that the One who had promised was faithful" (Hebrews 11:11, HCSB). Sarah's renewed faith in God was rewarded.

[Jesus instructs:] [7] *"Keep asking, and it will be given to you. Keep searching, and you will find. Keep knocking, and the door will be opened to you.* [8] *For everyone who asks receives, and the one who searches finds, and to the one who knocks, the door will be opened.*

Matthew 7:7-8, HCSB

Take delight in the LORD, and He will give you your heart's desires.

PSALM 37:4, HCSB

Session Four

4. We all live with unmet needs and unfulfilled desires. What two unique approaches for getting what we need from God are highlighted in Matthew 7 and Proverbs 37? How are these approaches complementary?

5. How can we reconcile the promises in Matthew 7:7-8 and Psalm 37:4 with Sarah's experience? Share a story from your own life about God opening a door or giving you your heart's desire.

Principle for Living

We sometimes stop expecting God's greatest blessings for our lives. Yet, He invites you to keep on seeking Him and searching for your fulfillment in Him alone. Your journey may be a struggle—even over the long haul—but as you delight in the Lord, you'll find the journey sweeter and at the "appointed times" He will give you the His good gifts.

CONNECTING - *15-20 Minutes*

LEADER: Use "Connecting" as a time to develop closeness within your group. Encourage and support one another as you face struggles on your journeys. Invite everyone to join in; ask them to be open and set the tone for openness by being the first to share your story.

GOD RESTORES OUR LOSSES

Sarah had many years of barrenness in her life, but as she held God's laughter—little Isaac—in her arms, all of that was replaced by enduring joy. In Genesis 21:6, she invites us to look at the way God worked in her life so we can laugh or delight in God too.

The prophet Joel lived in Judah during a time of devastation and suffering. He dedicated his ministry to calling the people of Judah back to repentance and commitment to God. God gave Joel a promise to share with His devastated people. Take comfort in this promise.

²⁵ *I [God] will restore the years that the swarming locust has eaten, the crawling locust, the consuming locust, and the chewing locust. ²⁶ You shall eat in plenty and be satisfied, and praise the name of the Lord your God, Who has dealt wondrously with you; and My people shall never be put to shame.*

JOEL 2:25-26, NKJV

Locusts are ravenous, devouring life as they swarm. In this passage, locusts represent the torment or consequences that have come into our lives as a result of bad decisions we or other people have made. They represent the pain and struggles that have chewed up our lives and relationships.

1. What does God promise in Joel 2:25-26 that He will do with the losses and devastation in your life? What degree of restoration does He describe? How much do you think is possible in this life?

LEADER INSTRUCTIONS FOR THE GROUP EXPERIENCE: Bring a DVD of While You Were Sleeping, *which stars Sandra Bullock and Bill Pullman. Set up a DVD player before the meeting. Read the following introduction and then show Scene 19, "A Second Chance," (on the DVD timer from 1:25:53 to 1:31:05, ending with the words: "He didn't want me"). Discuss questions 2-5.*

In the romantic comedy *While you Were Sleeping*, Lucy (Sandra Bullock) is a lonely subway worker with no family, who becomes smitten with a tall handsome stranger named Peter. She saves his life when he's mugged and falls into a coma. Through a set of mix-ups, she ends up posing as Peter's fiance. The whole scheme to marry Peter and escape her life becomes complicated when Lucy falls in love with Peter's brother Jack.

2. In the film, Lucy has schemed to get Peter to marry her. What are the things she's looking to gain? Peter can provide all these things, but what will she still lack if she goes through with the wedding?

3. What would Lucy risk if she dropped her scheme and trusted God to give her the deepest desires of her heart? What does she stand to gain if Jack (and God) comes through for her?

4. Describe a need or desire in your life for which you are still waiting on God. What are some things you've tried to speed up the process for God?

5. What have you learned about God from your times of waiting or struggle? What have you learned about yourself and your natural responses to frustration or adversity?

Share and record group prayer requests that you will regularly pray over between now and the next session. Also pray together today, asking God to pour an abundance of blessings into the lives of all group participants. Thank Him in advance for all the wonderful things He will do in each life.

PRAYER REQUESTS:

TAKING IT HOME

LEADER: For this week's "Taking It Home" questions, encourage group members to again retreat to a place that's special to each of them for their time with God. Perhaps there's a special mountain, trail, river, garden, or building. For some a bubble bath or sunroom will fit the bill. Be sure to highlight the importance of writing down thoughts, feelings, and key insights that God reveals. Journaling is a powerful tool for healing and change.

A QUESTION TO TAKE TO MY HEART

The following question asks you to look into your heart and focus on your deepest feelings about yourself. Our behaviors are the best indicators of what we really believe deep down. Look deep into the underlying beliefs in your heart where your truest attitudes and motivations live. Spend some time in reflecting, and don't settle for a quick answer.

In what areas of my life am I settling for second-best blessings? What heart desires have I not yet turned over to God? Why?

Session Four

A Question to Take to God

When you ask God a question, expect His Spirit to guide your heart in His truth. Be careful not to rush or manufacture an answer. Don't write down what you think the "right answer" is. Don't turn the Bible into a reference book or spiritual encyclopedia. Just pose a question to God and wait on Him. Remember, the litmus test for anything we hear form God is alignment with the Bible as our ultimate source of truth. Keep a journal of the insights you gain from your time with God.

   ξ *As I've struggled with disappointments in my life, God, where have You been? What do you want to say to me that will give me hope or help me to press on and delight in You?*

Scripture Notes

GENESIS 17:1-9,15-21; 18:1,6-15; 21:1-7

17:1 God Almighty. A translation of the Hebrew *El- Shaddai* which can mean "God Almighty," or "God, the Mountain One." *live in My presence and be devout.* God called Abram to a life of faith. The sign of his faith was his obedience. Abram had to be patient and wait for God to fulfill His promise of a son and an heir. Trying to fulfill that promise in his own way (through Hagar and Ishmael) had only resulted in pain and disaster.

17:2 I will establish My covenant. What God promised, He would do. God also made covenants with Noah (9:8-17) and with David (2 Sam. 7:5-16).

17:4-6 Abraham was the father not only of the Israelites, but also of the Ishmaelites, the Edomites, and the Midianites. Spiritually, he is the father of all believers. (Galatians 3:7)

17:5 Abram ... Abraham. The name Abram means, "father is exalted" or "high father," while Abraham means, "father of many" or "father of nations." This name was a sign of special favor with God and showed God's covenant promise.

17:6 will make nations and kings come from you. God's promise of increase of offspring, as mentioned in verse 2.

17:7 an everlasting covenant. God would always keep His end of the bargain. *your God.* God would stand by His people as their leader and provider. God later repeats this promise to Moses as part of His message to the Israelites.

17:8 eternal possession. Canaan would belong to Abraham's descendants permanently, as long as they continued in obedience.

17:9 keep My covenant. God assigned a condition for Abraham and his descendants: obedience.

17:15 Sarai ... Sarah. Sarai and Sarah both mean "princess," but as with Abraham, the name change was a sign of God's favor and God's promise that she would be the mother of many.

17:16 a son by her. Not through Hagar or any other person, but through Sarah this son would be born. Isaac was this promised son (21:1-7).

17:17 Abraham ... laughed. This was his reaction to the seeming impossibility of the promise. God then names him Isaac (v. 19), which means, "he laughs."

17:21 But I will confirm My covenant with Isaac. God reminded Abraham that His covenant would be with the son Abraham and Sarah would have and not with Ishmael, the son born to Abraham but not to Sarah.

17:22 God withdrew from Abraham. The Lord concluded their meeting as He did during a later visit to Abraham (18:33) and after a confrontation with Aaron and Miriam (Num. 12:9).

18:2 three men. It's obvious these were not ordinary visitors. The context would suggest that two of them were angels and the third was the Lord. The hospitality Abraham showed the three men was customary for the day. He immediately took care of his guests.

18:6 bread. This is not a loaf of bread as we would imagine it. The Hebrew word suggests more than one loaf. What Sarah baked for the guests was a basketful of flat unleavened bread common to that area. Our pita bread is similar to what was served.

18:12 laughed. Unable to contain her disbelief, Sarah quietly chuckled to herself. The thought of conceiving a child at her advanced age was a joke.

18:14 Is anything impossible for the LORD? It is clear that this is a rhetorical question. Then and now, whatever God wants to do, He will do. What a wonderful truth for God's people to ponder when we face tasks that seem impossible.

21:1 did ... what He had promised. Finally, the impossible promise came true (15:4; 17:15-19).

21:3 Isaac. The name means, "he laughs." Abraham once laughed, scoffing at the idea of fathering a son at his age (17:17). Sarah had laughed, too (18:12). This time, the laughter was happier.

21:5 100 years old. God promised Abraham, now 100 years old, that he would be the father of a son by Sarah (17:16-17).

MATTHEW 7:7-8

7:7-8 asking ... searching ... knocking. It is assumed these will be done from the perspective of the faith of one who is seeking first the kingdom (6:33). When we seek the kingdom, God answers our requests for our needs. This is not to say God will grant requests made out of the greed of one who seeks self-enhancement, but initiative and perseverance play an important role.

JOEL 2:25-26

2:25-26 locusts has eaten. Locusts are ravenous, devouring life as they swarm. In this passage, locusts represent the torment or consequences that have come to Israel as a result of bad decisions they have made. We can apply this in our lives to situations we have brought upon ourselves or other people have brought. They represent the pain and struggles that have chewed up our lives and relationships.

THE ROLLERCOASTER RIDE OF EMOTIONS

In Session Four, we reengaged with Sarah's life 13 years after Ishmael was born. After so many years, it seemed like she'd been left out of God's plan for Abraham's legacy. In trying to rush ahead of God, Sarah and Abraham got what they wanted—a son, but they did not receive the fullness of the blessing that God had promised. In settling for a second-best blessing, they stopped expecting God's best. Thankfully, God loved them and honored His promises even with their failings and the messiness of their lives. The miraculous birth of Isaac redeemed all the barren years in Sarah's life.

Although Sarah and Hagar have both seen God work in powerful and miraculous ways in their own lives, they still get swept away by a rollercoaster of emotions. As emotions overshadow trust, both women desperately need a fresh encounter with God.

B R E A K I N G   T H E   I C E - *10-15 Minutes*

LEADER INSTRUCTIONS FOR THE GROUP EXPERIENCE:
Allow group members about 5 minutes to work individually on the first set of "Breaking the Ice" questions. Draw the group back together to enable women to share their responses. This should be a fun way to launch into the discussion of emotions. Discuss the remaining questions as a group.

1. We're going to stretch our creative muscles today with a quick writing exercise. It involves using all five senses to describe various emotions.

   - In your opinion, what color is joy?

   - If anger had an odor, what would it smell like?

   - What is the sound of peace?

   - If jealousy had a texture, what would it feel like?

   - What does fear taste like?

2. How wild is the rollercoaster of emotions in your life? Share an example.

3. What insights did you gain this week as you opened a dialog with your heart about settling for second-best blessings? What did you hear from God about the disappointments in your life?

DISCOVERING THE TRUTH

25-30 Minutes

LEADER: For "Discovering the Truth," ask various group members to read the Bible passages aloud. The session today highlights the blow-up that occurs in Abraham's household and God's cleanup of the emotional and spiritual fallout. Keep things moving at a steady pace so you leave time for the "Embracing the Truth" questions and the "Connecting" group experience.

THE BLOW-UP

Sarah certainly knew what jealousy felt like. Ever since the day she decided to supplant God's perfect plan, Sarah struggled with envy and wounded pride. When the internal chaos brought about by her poor choices finally erupted, it resulted in tragedy.

[8] The child grew and was weaned, and Abraham held a great feast on the day Isaac was weaned. [9] But Sarah saw the son mocking—the one Hagar the Egyptian had borne to Abraham. [10] So she said to Abraham, "Drive out this slave with her son, for the son of this slave will not be a co-heir with my son Isaac!" [11] Now this was a very difficult thing for Abraham because of his son. [12] But God said to Abraham, "Do not be concerned about the boy and your slave. Whatever Sarah says to you, listen to her, because your offspring will be traced through Isaac. [13] But I will also make a nation of the slave's son because he is your offspring."

GENESIS 21:8-13, HCSB

LEADER: Discuss as many discovery questions as time permits. It will help to highlight in advance the questions you don't want to miss. Be familiar with the Scripture Notes at the end of this session.

1. What do you think was behind the teenager Ishmael's response to his younger half-brother during his weaning celebration?

2. What do Sarah's words about Hagar and Ishmael in verse 10 indicate about her relationship with them over the past 14-15 years? From her words and actions, what do think is really getting to Sarah?

3. Why would God allow Sarah to force Hagar and Ishmael from their home? How does He plan to redeem this difficult situation for both women and their children?

4. Anger is often a reaction to deep hurt or a sense of betrayal. How do you imagine Sarah's feelings as a wife and mother entered into her outburst? How did God respond to Sarah? What does this indicate about God's understanding of the human condition?

Despite all God had done to bless Sarah, she still struggled with her feelings. Sarah did what so many of us do when times get tough and our feelings get hurt. She stuffed her feelings deep inside rather than dealing with them in a healthy way. Ishmael's latest offense was enough to send Sarah beyond her boiling point. While Sarah was once eager to embrace Ishmael as her own son, she seemed to have no remorse over sentencing him to what could have been a long and miserable death in the wilderness.

Principle for Living
Your feelings are a God-given gift that can bring deep joy or signal problems that need to be addressed. When feelings are dealt with in healthy ways, relationships can be reconciled. But if you ignore or misuse emotions, you can allow problems to fester and rot the heart of relationships.

INVITED INTO THE LARGER STORY

In Genesis 16:11, before the boy was born, God instructed Hagar to name her son Ishmael, which means "God hears." As so often happens with us, Hagar seems to have forgotten God's dramatic rescue years before and the ongoing reminder that God sees and God hears—*Ishmael*.

[14] Early in the morning Abraham got up, took bread and a waterskin, put them on Hagar's shoulders, and sent her and the boy away. She left and wandered in the Wilderness of Beer-sheba. [15] When the water in the skin was gone, she left the boy under one of the bushes. [16] Then she went and sat down nearby, about a bowshot away, for she said, "I can't bear to watch the boy die!" So as she sat nearby, she wept loudly. [17] God heard the voice of the boy, and the angel of God called to Hagar from heaven and said to her, "What's wrong, Hagar? Don't be afraid, for God has heard the voice of the boy from the place where he is. [18] Get up, help the boy up, and sustain him, for I will make him a great nation." [19] Then God opened her eyes, and she saw a well of water. So she went and filled the waterskin and gave the boy a drink. [20] God was with the boy, and he grew; he settled in the wilderness and became an archer. [21] He settled in the Wilderness of Paran, and his mother got a wife for him from the land of Egypt.

GENESIS 21:14-21, HCSB

5. Hagar was again in the desert and times were desperate. How did she respond to this struggle in her life and to her fear (verses 15-16)? Who did God hear cry out to Him this time (verse 17)?

6. When God came to Hagar's rescue years before, He opened her eyes to His total involvement in her life. In a broader sense, to what did God open her eyes this time?

7. What did God ask of Hagar once He opened her eyes? Why do you think He didn't just complete the full rescue in His own power?

The last time Hagar was rejected and abandoned, God began to open her eyes to reveal His presence and protection. Yet now — in one of the darkest times of her life — as she contemplates her precious son's death, Hagar didn't pray to God or call on Him for help. Instead, her fear overpowered her trust in God and she broke down — mirroring another tendency with which many of us struggle. God recognized Hagar's struggles and her need for divine intervention. Taking Hagar a step deeper in her journey of faith, God opens her eyes to the greater reality that surrounds her, including His long-range plans as well as the resources He's put at her disposal.

Principle for Living
Even when you're unable to cry out to God, He is still the God who hears.
While He <u>will</u> come to your rescue, He also wants
to open you eyes to larger story and to the resources He has provided
so that you can join Him in His redemptive mission.

EMBRACING THE TRUTH
15-20 Minutes

LEADER: This section focuses on helping group members integrate what they've learned from the Bible into their own hearts and lives. Questions will lead the group to discuss suffering and injustice in our own lives. Invite volunteers to read the Bible passages aloud.

A NEW SET OF EYES

Were Hagar and Ishmael just an abandoned slave and an illegitimate child? Not in God's eyes. God had a purpose and a plan for them that no amount of sin or family turmoil could erase. He had to open Hagar's eyes to see their sufferings in light of His redemptive master plan.

We all struggle with the age old question: "Why is there so much suffering in this life?" Like Sarah and Hagar, we struggle to make sense of emotional pain and deal with it in our own ways.

1. Discuss some ways that people tend to deal with hurt, rejection, injustice and other suffering in their lives.

Some of those closest to Jesus when He walked the earth — His apostles — experienced a great deal of suffering, mistreatment, and hurt. Paul learned so much from God in his own sufferings about how God uses the difficulties in our lives, whether they come from our own decisions, from the choices of other people, from attacks by the Enemy, or directly from the hand of God.

[25] But if we hope for what we do not see, with perseverance we wait eagerly for it. [26] In the same way the Spirit also helps our weakness; for we do not know how to pray as we should, but the Spirit Himself intercedes for us with groanings too deep for words; [27] and He who searches the hearts knows what the mind of the Spirit is, because He intercedes for the saints according to the will of God. [28] And we know that God causes all things to work together for good to those who love God, to those who are called according to His purpose.

ROMANS 8:25-28, NASB

2. According to Romans 8:25-28, where is God when we're suffering and struggling? How does it change your perspective or feelings to know that it's not all up to you to make things right and take care of yourself?

3. In what ways does the truth of Romans 8:28 open our eyes to the larger picture of what God is doing? What attitudes would you expect to see in a person who fully lived the promise of verse 28?

[3] And not only that, but we also rejoice in our afflictions, because we know that affliction produces endurance, [4] endurance produces proven character, and proven character produces hope. [5] This hope does not disappoint, because God's love has been poured out in our hearts through the Holy Spirit who was given to us.

ROMANS 5:3-5, HCSB

4. What purpose for suffering does Paul highlight in Romans 5:3-5? Why would God want us to rejoice even in times of affliction? (See Romans 5:5 and 8:25,28.)

¹⁵ For you did not receive a spirit that makes you a slave again to fear, but you received the Spirit of sonship. And by him we cry, "Abba, Father." ¹⁶ The Spirit himself testifies with our spirit that we are God's children. ¹⁷ Now if we are children, then we are heirs — heirs of God and co-heirs with Christ, if indeed we share in his sufferings in order that we may also share in his glory. ¹⁸ I consider that our present sufferings are not worth comparing with the glory that will be revealed in us.

ROMANS 8:15-18, NIV

5. We like Sarah and Hagar can become slaves to our fears. According to Romans 8:15-18, what is your true identity and how should that affect the way you respond to struggles and suffering?

Principle for Living

God made each of us for a purpose. Every moment, every experience has eternal significance. When you view your experiences — good or bad — as part of God's eternal purpose, you'll find peace even in the midst of turmoil.

God has a larger view of our lives than we do, and He is using all of our life experiences to shape us into His image. In the same way, we often can't see the influence that our attitudes, beliefs, and actions have on those around us, or on future generations. But God sees the long-term spiritual impact of our lives.

Hagar and Ishmael would survive the desert. And though they were cut off from Abraham's inheritance, they had a physical and spiritual inheritance through the Lord's blessing. "Indeed, Ishmael was destined to be the legendary ancestor of all the Bedouin tribes of northern Arabia." [1]

¹² Now these are the records of the generations of Ishmael, Abraham's son, whom Hagar the Egyptian, Sarah's maid, bore to Abraham; ¹³ and these are the names of the sons of Ishmael, by their names, in the order of their birth: Nebaioth, the firstborn of Ishmael, and Kedar and Adbeel and Mibsam ¹⁴ and Mishma and Dumah and Massa, ¹⁵ Hadad and Tema, Jetur, Naphish and Kedemah. ¹⁶ These are the sons of Ishmael and these are their names, by their villages, and by their camps; twelve princes according to their tribes.

GENESIS 25:12-16, NASB

Principle for Living

God's heart is always to redeem you, to give you "a crown of beauty instead of ashes, festive oil instead of mourning, and splendid clothes instead of despair" so you "will be called righteous trees, planted by the LORD, to glorify Him." (Isaiah 61:3) His glory is revealed in a mature woman who trusts in God no matter what her circumstances.

CONNECTING - *10-15 minutes*

LEADER: Use "Connecting" as a time to deepen relationships within the group and to help each woman connect with God in a more personal way.. Encourage and support one another through the trying times of life. Be sensitive to group members who are dealing with difficult life issues.

ASKING THE RIGHT QUESTIONS

An old proverb reminds us that "wisdom does not consist in having all the answers, but in asking the right questions." To illustrate: "Why me?" is often a futile question. We seldom discover an answer for it. There are, however, valuable questions to ask when we find ourselves wandering in a wilderness of suffering and injustice:

- What character traits can God develop in me through this experience?
- How can I use this struggle to bring comfort and hope to others?
- How can God redeem or bring good out of this difficult time?
- What is God up to in the lives of those around me?
- How can God and I deepen our relationship in this time of struggle?

LEADER INSTRUCTIONS FOR THE GROUP EXPERIENCE: In advance of the meeting, purchase some scratch-art paper from a local art supplier or by searching for "scratch-art paper" on the Internet. Crayola® has a similar product for children called Color Explosion™ or Discovery Paper.

Play worship music to create a pleasant setting for this exercise. For question 3, give each woman a piece of the scratch-art paper and a utensil or pen. Instruct each one to spend 5 minutes of quiet time with God to ask Him to show her how He has worked in her life through her most difficult times.

1. How does Romans 8:28 challenge us to examine our unhealed jealousy, disappointment, or bitterness? What are some ways that our unhealed emotions can cause pain in our lives? In the lives of others?

2. In what areas are you looking for a sense of purpose? How would your life be different if you lived every moment with one?

3. ACTIVITY: On the special paper provided by your group leader draw a picture representing the answer to this question:

How has God worked through your life's most difficult times?

Underneath the black surface you'll discover a rainbow of colors emerging under the pressure of your utensil or pen. Consider how God's power of redemption compares to the colors emerging from the paper's surface.

Take a few minutes together to share your drawings and stories.

Share and record group prayer requests that you will regularly pray over between now and the next session. Also pray together today, asking God to give each of you a new set of eyes to see your difficult times as part of a larger story, and to see that God's purpose is always to redeem your suffering.

PRAYER REQUESTS:

TAKING IT HOME

QUESTIONS TO TAKE TO MY HEART

This is introspection time—time to grapple with what drives your thinking and behavior. Strive to understand what you really believe in your innermost being about God, yourself, and the world in which you live. Your behavior—not your intellectual stance—is the best indicator of your truest beliefs in your innermost being (Psalm 51:6, NASB).

❧ *Which of my emotions tend to draw me closer to God? Which tend to drive me away from God?*

❧ *When I feel discouraged, which do I tend to doubt more: God's power to accomplish His purposes or God's love for me? What's really behind those doubts?*

Session Five

QUESTIONS TO TAKE TO GOD

When you ask God a question, expect His Spirit to guide your heart in His truth. Be careful not to rush or manufacture an answer. Don't write down what you think the "right answer" is. Don't turn the Bible into a reference book or spiritual encyclopedia. Just pose a question to God and wait on Him. Remember, the litmus test for anything we hear form God is alignment with the Bible as our ultimate source of truth. Keep a journal of the insights you gain from your time with God.

❦ *My dear God who hears and sees me, what is it that You need to open my eyes to see about You? About my relationships? About the mission and resources You've laid out before me?*

Scripture Notes

GENESIS 21:8-21; 25:12-16

21: 8 was weaned. The weaning time usually occurred between a child's second and third birthday. Due to high rates of infant mortality in those days, it was not uncommon to plan a big celebration on the day that a child reached his weaning age. It indicated that he stood a good chance of survival.

21:9 the one Hagar ... had borne. This refers to Ishmael.

21:10 slave with her son. Sarah didn't want her son to share his inheritance. This act was considered wrong in their culture. Ishmael was in essence cut off from Abraham's inheritance.

21:11 difficult thing for Abraham. Abraham clearly cared for his son Ishmael. He was greatly concerned that Ishmael would have a very difficult life being the estranged son of a servant woman.

21:12 Whatever Sarah says to you. Once again God set Abraham straight, promising that both sons, Isaac and Ishmael, would father great nations. Even so, God's plan for Abraham's descendants would unfold through Isaac's line, regardless of the pain his disobedient servants were causing themselves in the process.

21:14 Early in the morning. Despite certain anxiety, Abraham obeyed God's command immediately, even though it meant being away from Ishmael. *Beersheba* means "well of seven" or "well of swearing."

21:17 God heard ... God has heard. The name Ishmael means, "God hears."

21:19 God opened her eyes. Hagar's grief was so deep that God had to open her eyes so she could see the much-needed water. The Old Testament often uses a spring or water well to symbolize both spiritual and physical salvation. "God didn't create a new source of water. He simply opened her eyes to see what was already present. When we are in despair God very seldom needs to create something new to deliver us. Most often He simply opens our eyes to see the spiritual and other resources that are all around us." *The 365-Day Devotional Commentary* by Lawrence O. Richards (Colorado Springs, CO.: ChariotVictor Publishing, 1990.

21:21 his mother got a wife for him from the land of Egypt. Hagar made sure Ishmael married one of her kind. "The last glimpse we have of Hagar is of her securing a wife for her son, out of the land of Egypt, her own land — the land of idols and worldliness. Untaught by the piety and instruction of Abraham, and by God's mercy to herself, Hagar failed Him in the choice of such a wife for the boy whom He had blessed." *All the Women of the Bible* by Herbert Lockyer, p. 63.

ROMANS 5:3-5; 8:15-18, 25-28

5:3 afflictions. Literally, "pressure" or "tribulation." What is in view is not sorrow or pain, but the negative reaction of an unbelieving world. In New Testament times, suffering was the normal and expected lot of Christians (Acts 14:22). Thus, suffering was seen as a sign of true Christianity (2 Thess. 1:4-5). *endurance.* Fortitude or determination. The word describes the active overcoming of misfortune, rather than mere passive acceptance.

5:4 character. A word used of metal that has been so heated by fire that all the impurities are removed. *hope.* The confidence born out of suffering that God is indeed transforming one's character, and that He will keep on doing so until the person is glorified.

8:15 spirit of slavery. The Holy Spirit brings us, not into a new form of anxious bondage, but rather unites us with Christ, enabling each of us to share in His sonship. *you received.* The verb tense indicates that this is a one-time, past action—something that happened at conversion. *spirit of adoption.* The Roman practice of adoption was a most serious and complicated process, because a child was the absolute possession of his father. For a child to be adopted into a new family, he was first symbolically "sold" by his father to the adopting father. Then the legal case for adoption was taken to the magistrate. *cry.* In the Psalms this word is used of urgent prayer (e.g. Ps. 3:4). *Abba.* An Aramaic word used by children; best translated "Daddy," signifying a close, intimate relationship. *Abba, Father.* The very words Jesus prayed in the Garden of Gethsemane (Mark 14:36).

8:16 The Spirit himself testifies. In the Roman adoptive proceedings there were several witnesses to the ceremony who would, if a dispute arose later, verify that the particular child had actually been adopted. The Holy Spirit is the One who verifies a person's adoption into the family of God.

8:17 heirs. If someone is one of God's children, then that person is an heir, and will share in God's riches. In fact, Jesus is God's true heir (v. 3), but since believers are "in Christ," they become sons and daughters of God by adoption and thus are joint-heirs with Christ.

8:28 all things to work together. It is God who takes that which is adverse and painful (the groans, the persecution, and even death—vv. 35-36) and brings profit out of it. *for good to those who love God.* This does not mean things work out so that believers preserve their comfort and convenience. Rather, such action on God's part enables these difficult experiences to assist in the process of salvation and growth. *who are called according to His* purpose. The love people have for God is a reflection of the fact and reality of God's love for them as expressed in His call to individuals to follow Christ. A person's love for God has been said to be a proof of God's love for that person. If God had not called an individual, that person would still be His enemy, unable and unwilling to love Him.

SESSION QUOTATIONS

1. *Great People of the Bible and How They Lived* (Pleasantville, NY: The Reader's Digest Association, 1974), p. 42.

STREAMS IN THE DESERT

LEADER: Try to bring a piece of cross-stitching, either something you're working on or a piece you've removed from its frame. Turn the piece so only the back is visible to group members as they arrive. Use this to illustrate the point in this session's introduction.

Through our study of the entangled lives of Sarah and Hagar, we've examined nearly everything the Bible tells us about these women. We've seen the good, the bad, and the ugly. In Session Five, we saw them continue, even as older women, to struggle with issues in their spiritual lives. Somehow we take comfort that these weak, very human women were chosen by God to mother great nations. It means that our Father can use us in amazing ways in our day ... even though at times we're far from perfect children.

You've heard the old cliché, "Beauty is in the eye of the beholder." When you look at the back side of a piece of cross-stitching, all you can see is a jumble of threads and knots. Nothing beautiful there. But if you'll turn the piece over and look at the front, you'll often find a beautiful, smooth, and complete picture. Sometimes beauty is visible only when we look at the finished product. In our final session, as we read about Sarah's death, let's examine her life from an eternal perspective.

BREAKING THE ICE - *15-20 Minutes*

LEADER: These "Breaking the Ice" questions will open the dialog about our dreams and our legacies. Keep this light-hearted.

Sometimes it can be fun to look back at the past and laugh at ourselves.

1. What's the worst fashion trend you remember from your teenage years?

2. What personal dream or expectation did you have that you are now thrilled or at least relieved to know did *not* work out?

Session Six

3. Pretend you're 18 again. What questions would you like to ask your adult self about how your life has turned out? What about the you-of-today would the you-of-age-18 be surprised (and pleased) to learn?

4. In your reflection time this week, what did you discover about your emotions, your doubts, and your relationship with God?

5. What did you hear from God this week? Has He opened your eyes during the course of this study to any particular new insights about Him, your relationships, your identity, or your purpose?

DISCOVERING THE TRUTH
20-25 Minutes

LEADER: For "Discovering the Truth," ask various group members to read the extended Bible passage aloud (if you're concerned about time, read only Genesis 23:1-6 and 17-21). The group will focus on the lasting impacts of our lives. Be sure to leave time for the "Embracing the Truth" and "Connecting" segments that follow this discussion.

LOOK AT THE LARGER STORY

1. On what bases do you think most people in our culture judge the value of a person's life? How about within the church community?

John MacArthur sums up well the picture that we *could* hold in our minds of Sarah's life from the glimpses the Bible gives: "She could throw fits and tantrums. She knew how to be manipulative. And she was even known to be mean. At one time or another, she exemplified almost every trait associated with the caricature of a churlish woman. She could be impatient, temperamental, conniving, cantankerous, cruel, flighty, pouty, jealous, erratic, unreasonable, a whiner, a complainer, or a nag." [1]

2. How would you like to be remembered by your family, friends, and co-workers? What's your opinion of Sarah after studying parts of her story?

Our lives are a lot like a piece of cross-stitched fabric viewed from the back. In our culture, we often judge the value of a people's lives based on the mistakes they've made and their publicized failures. We tend to measure people by their worst days rather than their best. Likewise, we see our own lives as a series of knots and jumbled thread—a mess. But God has a purpose and plan for each life, and it can only be correctly measured by looking at it from a proper eternal perspective. Let's look at the end of Sarah's life ...

[1] *Now Sarah lived 127 years; these were all the years of her life.* [2] *Sarah died in Kiriath-arba (that is, Hebron) in the land of Canaan, and Abraham went in to mourn for Sarah and to weep for her.*

[3] *Then Abraham got up from beside his dead wife and spoke to the Hittites:* [4] *"I am a resident alien among you. Give me a burial site among you so that I can bury my dead."*

[5] *The Hittites replied to Abraham,* [6] *"Listen to us, lord. You are God's chosen one among us. Bury your dead in our finest burial place. None of us will withhold from you his burial place for burying your dead."*

[7] *Then Abraham rose and bowed down to the Hittites, the people of the land.* [8] *He said to them, "If you are willing for me to bury my dead, listen to me and ask Ephron son of Zohar on my behalf* [9] *to give me the cave of Machpelah that belongs to him; it is at the end of his field. Let him give it to me in your presence, for the full price, as a burial place."*

[10] *Ephron was present with the Hittites. So in the presence of all the Hittites who came to the gate of his city, Ephron the Hittite answered Abraham:* [11] *"No, my lord. Listen*

to me. I give you the field, and I give you the cave that is in it. I give it to you in the presence of my people. Bury your dead." [12] Abraham bowed down to the people of the land [13] and said to Ephron in the presence of the people of the land, "Please listen to me. Let me pay the price of the field. Accept it from me, and let me bury my dead there."

[14] Ephron answered Abraham and said to him, [15] "My lord, listen to me. Land worth 400 shekels of silver—what is that between you and me? Bury your dead." [16] Abraham agreed with Ephron, and Abraham weighed out to Ephron the silver that he had agreed to in the hearing of the Hittites: 400 shekels of silver at the current commercial rate. [17] So Ephron's field at Machpelah near Mamre—the field with its cave and all the trees anywhere within the boundaries of the field—became [18] Abraham's possession in the presence of all the Hittites who came to the gate of his city. [19] After this, Abraham buried his wife Sarah in the cave of the field at Machpelah near Mamre (that is, Hebron) in the land of Canaan.

[20] The field with its cave passed from the Hittites to Abraham as a burial place.

GENESIS 23:1-20, HCSB

LEADER: Encourage participation by inviting different individuals to respond. Be familiar with the Scripture Notes at the end of this session.

3. Why did the Hittites so graciously respond to Abraham's request to bury Sarah on their land? How does it seem they felt about Abraham and Sarah (see verses 4-6)?

4. What is the significance of Abraham's referring to himself as "a resident alien" in Canaan and especially his ownership of land in Canaan? (Hint: Refer to God's promises in Genesis 15:13-21.)

5. Isaac was born when Sarah was well past her child-bearing years at 90, but verse 1 says, "Sarah lived 127 years." Do the math and discuss how much Sarah was able to invest in raising her "son of the promise."

6. As you read Abraham's words in verses 2-4, how did Abraham view his wife? Given what you know about Sarah, what positive traits do you see in her as a wife, mother, and woman in general?

The Apostle Peter, who as a young follower of Jesus was forceful and impetuous, learned a great deal from Jesus' example about living a gentle, humble life. He wrote to the early church husbands about treating their wives with understanding and honor. He instructed wives about living with purity and respect toward their husbands. See who he identifies as a model wife.

[To wives:] 3 Your adornment must not be merely external—braiding the hair, and wearing gold jewelry, or putting on dresses; 4 but let it be the hidden person of the heart, with the imperishable quality of a gentle and quiet spirit, which is precious in the sight of God. 5 For in this way in former times the holy women also, who hoped in God, used to adorn themselves, being submissive to their own husbands; 6 just as Sarah obeyed Abraham, calling him lord, and you have become her children if you do what is right without being frightened by any fear.

1 PETER 3:3-6, NASB

7. How does the Bible look back on Sarah? According to 1 Peter 3:3-6, what key traits does she model for us as the mother of the nation of Israel and the spiritual mother of all Christ-followers?

Perhaps now we see Sarah, our independent princess with her obvious flaws, in a new light. Although there were ups and downs throughout her life, she was a woman of gentleness, perseverance, and faithfulness. She stood by her husband with deep affection and respect. She loved God and ultimately trusted her entire life to His often difficult plan. She finished life strong, revered in 1 Peter 3:4 as possessing *"the imperishable quality of a gentle and quiet spirit, which is precious in the sight of God."* Now she stands face-to-face with the God whom she trusted despite so many uncertainties, difficult life situations, and her own human weaknesses. Sarah's journey in this life may be over, but her influence lives on. Hebrews 11, the "Faith Hall of Fame," celebrates steadfastness and faith as her enduring legacy: *"since she considered that the One who had promised was faithful."*

Principle for Living

Never give up and lose heart, even when life becomes difficult.
The life of God's children is characterized by staying in the race and finishing
strong. Ask God to empower you with the qualities He finds precious
in Sarah: a gentle and quiet spirit, a heart that does what is right rather than
giving in to fears, and perhaps most of all ... a deep trust in God.

EMBRACING THE TRUTH
15-20 Minutes

LEADER: This section focuses on helping group members integrate what they've learned from the Bible into their own hearts and lives. Invite volunteers to read the explanations and Bible passages.

STAY ON THE JOURNEY

God redeemed *every* part of Sarah's life—her successes and failures; God used her in a vital way to further His plan of redemption for all mankind. In the end, Sarah is rightfully remembered as a faithful woman and an example of godliness for future generations. Her secret was staying on the journey that God had laid out for her regardless of setbacks or even disasters.

Sarah and Hagar both demonstrate that God sees success not based on our tally sheets of accomplishments and failures, but based upon faithfulness to our journey with Him. Paul, in his letter to the Philippians, compares the spiritual journey to the process of running a race.

¹² I'm not saying that I have this all together, that I have it made. But I am well on my way, reaching out for Christ, who has so wondrously reached out for me. ¹³ Friends, don't get me wrong: By no means do I count myself an expert in all of this, but I've got my eye on the goal, where God is beckoning us onward—to Jesus. ¹⁴ I'm off and running, and I'm not turning back.

PHILIPPIANS 3:12-14, THE MESSAGE

1. What attitudes and emotions come through in Paul's words? As you take an honest look at your own heart, how does your passion for Jesus measure against Paul's?

2. What does Paul highlight as the motivations for his passion? Why do you think we lose sight of these motivations in our own lives?

3. Why is forgetting what lies behind a necessary part of growing in spiritual maturity? Why do we so often have trouble forgetting what's behind us and focusing on the goal of pressing onward toward Jesus?

Principle for Living

Knowing our ultimate purpose in life frees us from so much anxiety, confusion, and wasted time. Our ultimate purpose is to deeply love and glorify God and to find joy and pleasure in Him. A related purpose is to love and serve others.

DO NOT LOSE HEART IN THE DESERTS!

Sarah and Hagar failed frequently, fell down spiritually many times, and were knocked off their feet at times by life's trials. The reason they finished strong was because they got back up and pressed on.

Above all else, guard your heart, for it is the wellspring of life.

PROVERBS 4:23, NIV

[Jesus invites us:] [37] *"If anyone is thirsty, let him come to Me and drink.* [38] *"He who believes in Me, as the Scripture said, 'From his innermost being will flow rivers of living water.'"* [39] *But this He spoke of the Spirit, whom those who believed in Him were to receive; for the Spirit was not yet given, because Jesus was not yet glorified.*

JOHN 7:37B-39, NASB

4. Why would Proverbs 4 warn us to guard our hearts "above all else"? What powerful ally do we now have who was not available before Jesus?

In his second letter to the Corinthians, Paul's gives us vital insights to help us effectively deal with pain, failures, and suffering, Peter elaborates on this same theme.

16 Therefore we do not lose heart, but though our outer man is decaying, yet our inner man is being renewed day by day. 17 For momentary, light affliction is producing for us an eternal weight of glory far beyond all comparison, 18 while we look not at the things which are seen, but at the things which are not seen; for the things which are seen are temporal, but the things which are not seen are eternal.

2 CORINTHIANS 4:16-18, NASB

3 Praise be to the God and Father of our Lord Jesus Christ! In his great mercy he has given us new birth into a living hope through the resurrection of Jesus Christ from the dead, 4 and into an inheritance that can never perish, spoil or fade—kept in heaven for you, 5 who through faith are shielded by God's power until the coming of the salvation that is ready to be revealed in the last time. 6 In this you greatly rejoice, though now for a little while you may have had to suffer grief in all kinds of trials. 7 These have come so that your faith—of greater worth than gold, which perishes even though refined by fire—may be proved genuine and may result in praise, glory and honor when Jesus Christ is revealed.

1 PETER 1:3-7, NIV

5. In what ways can our failures and trials help to "refine" our faith (1 Peter 1:7; 2 Corinthians 4:17)?

6. On what do both Paul and Peter tell us to keep as our focus (2 Corinthians 4:17-18; 1 Peter 1:3-5)? Brainstorm ways that you can strengthen this ability individually and as a group of friends who support one another?

Session Six

Principle for Living
Especially in those desert times of your life, turn fully to Jesus to satisfy the deepest thirsts of your soul. Allow the living water to flow out of your innermost being where the Spirit now lives. Always guard your heart by fixing your hope on the unseen eternal reality and your glorious inheritance with Jesus.

CONNECTING - *10-15 Minutes*

LEADER INSTRUCTION FOR THIS EXPERIENCE: *Use "Connecting" as a time to encourage, and support one another. You will need a CD player, a worship CD, a large serving bowl, and a water pitcher for this exercise. You'll also need a broken construction paper chain, symbolizing the sins participants threw away in Session Two. For the third pass, you will need a small bag of sand available at arts and crafts stores.*

When we consider the messy situations that littered Sarah's life and the messes in our own, we can be thankful that God used her and will use us *in spite* of that messiness. However, the truth is that God loves us *in* and even *because of* our messiness. Amazingly, He actually uses our messiness as part of His redemptive plan in our lives and in the lives of others around us.

LIVING WATER IN THE DESERT

PASS 1: As worship music plays quietly, your leader will pass around an empty serving bowl. When the bowl comes to you, pray aloud: "Lord, help me to make sense of my barren times." Continue around the circle.

PASS 2: When the bowl gets back to the leader, she will place a broken construction-paper chain inside. This will symbolize the sins you released in Session Two. When the bowl comes to you this time, pray aloud: "Lord, help me to let go of my past failures."

PASS 3: When the bowl gets back to the leader, she will pour a bag of sand into it. This will represent the desert that Hagar faced as well as the dry times in our relationships with God. When the bowl comes to you, pray aloud: "Lord, help me to stay faithful in my desert times and to turn to You."

PASS 4: For the fourth part of this activity, the leader will pass around a pitcher of water. When the pitcher is passed to you, touch the actual water, and pray aloud: "Thank you, Holy Spirit, that Your presence in my heart is like never-ending wellspring of water to my parched soul. Help me to drink deeply and often."

Discuss your thoughts and feelings.

Session Six

Share and record group prayer requests that you will regularly pray over the next couple weeks. In addition to doing this, pray together that God will strengthen and encourage each participant as she takes her heart's deepest thirsts and questions to God this week.

PRAYER REQUESTS:

REDEMPTIVE PROLOGUE TO SARAH'S LIFE

On your own, take time to read the wonderfully redemptive words in beginning of Genesis 25. You'll see that Abraham lived to the ripe old age of 175. After the death of his beloved Sarah, he took another wife and fathered several other children.

The redemptive part of the story is that when Abraham died, his two sons Isaac and Ishmael were together as brothers and, in one accord, buried Abraham's body in cave of Machpelah right next to Sarah.

TAKING IT HOME

QUESTIONS TO TAKE TO MY HEART

The following question asks you to look into your heart and focus on your deepest feelings about yourself. Our behaviors are the best indicators of what we really believe in our innermost being. Look deep into the underlying beliefs in your heart where your truest attitudes and motivations live.

❧ *At which times in my life have I either lost heart or been tempted to give up? What innermost beliefs allowed my faith to be so shaken and also disconnected me from Jesus' living water?*

❧ *How well am I doing at "forgetting what lies behind" and pressing on in my journey with God? What have I been holding onto rather than releasing it to Jesus?*

Session Six

85

QUESTIONS TO TAKE TO GOD

When you ask God a question, expect His Spirit to guide your heart in His truth. Be careful not to rush or manufacture an answer. Don't write down what you think the "right answer" is. Don't turn the Bible into a reference book or spiritual encyclopedia. Just pose a question to God and wait on Him. Remember, the litmus test for anything we hear form God is alignment with the Bible as our ultimate source of truth. Keep a journal of the insights you gain from your time with God.

   ❧ *My Lover and My Redeemer, what is there in my life that You want to redeem?*

   ❧ *You commended Sarah's gentle and quite spirit and her faithfulness. What is it that You like about me? What is it in me that brings You delight and joy?*

Scripture Notes

GENESIS 23:1-20

23:1 Sarah lived 127 years. Sarah lived long enough to see her son, Isaac, reach adulthood.

23:3 Hittites. This tribe lived in the area of Hebron during this time. This would be one of the tribes driven out by the Hebrews (Josh. 3:10).

23:4 resident alien among you. Abraham was living in a land he knew would one day belong to his descendants. He never possessed the land; instead, he lived as a nomad and bought land in order to bury his beloved wife. Abraham was using this expression to bargain.

23:6 You are God's chosen one. The Hittites probably knew of Abraham's great wealth. Despite his nomadic lifestyle, he did own a great deal of livestock and had other forms of wealth.

23:9 cave of Machpelah. Although no one knows the exact location of this cave, according to tradition, it is beneath a Muslim shrine in Hebron.

23:10 who came to the gate. A city's primary gateway was the traditional place where important matters were settled. The exchange between Ephron and Abraham was traditional bargaining and took place in the hearing of many witnesses (v. 16).

23:14 No one really expected Abraham to accept the free offer of land in Hebron. This conversation between Abraham and Ephron is an example of the courteous, indirect negotiation style that was common in the Middle East. Ephron's suggested price of 400 shekels of silver was just a bargaining ploy. He would have expected Abraham to negotiate down to a more reasonable price. But Abraham does not try to negotiate, even though it is expectable and reasonable to do so. He is not interested in business matters at this point. He wants only to bury his beloved wife in the land that the Lord promised to them. (from *iLumina Gold*, Tyndale House Publishers, Inc., 1996)

23:15 Land worth 400 shekels. Ephron was acting as though his offer was generous, but 400 shekels was an extremely high price for such a property. Ephron seems to have been taking advantage of Abraham.

23:16 at the current commercial rate. Abraham paid the current correct amount, even though standards changed at various times.

23:17 field … cave … trees. Ephron managed to free himself of all his legal and financial obligations relating to the property by negotiating the sale not only of the cave of Machpelah (which is all Abraham really wanted) but the entire field and its contents. This is the only land Abraham ever really owned.

23:19 buried his wife. By establishing this "family plot" in Canaan, Abraham was expressing his deep faith in God's promise to give his descendants the land. Canaan was his home now and would be for a long time. Years later he would be buried here as well (25:10).

PHILIPPIANS 3:12-14

3:12 Not saying that I have this all together. He has not gained full possession of what Christ has for him. *have it made.* This is the only time in his letters that Paul uses this word, which means "fully mature". Paul indicates he has not yet fully understood Jesus Christ. There is simply too much to know of Christ ever to grasp it all this side of heaven. *on my way.* In contrast to those groups that claim it is possible to attain spiritual perfection here and now, the Christian life is one of relentless striving to know Christ in His fullness. *reaching out for Christ.* Winning a prize, as for example, in a race, or also to understand or comprehend something. *Christ, who has so wondrously reached out for me.* Paul refers here to his conversion experience on the Damascus Road.

3:13 I'm not turning back. In order to press on to a successful conclusion of his spiritual pilgrimage, Paul must first cease looking at what he has accomplished or failed to do in the past. *beckoning us onward.* If the first movement in the spiritual pilgrimage is to forget the past, the second is to concentrate totally on what lies ahead—full comprehension of Jesus Christ.

3:14 eye on the goal. The mark on the track that signifies the end of the race. What Paul seems to have in mind is the moment at the end of the race, when the winner is called forward by the games master to receive the victory palm or wreath.

1 PETER 1:3-7; 3:1-6

1:3 new birth. When people accept Jesus as Savior, something so radical happens that they can be said to be reborn into a whole new life. *a living hope.* This is the first thing new birth brings. Specifically here, their hope is that one day when Christ comes again they will experience the full fruit of salvation. *the resurrection of Jesus Christ.* This is the means of a believer's salvation and the foundation of his faith.

1:4 into an inheritance. To be born again means they have become part of a new family, and like all sons and daughters they can expect an inheritance. *imperishable, uncorrupted, and unfading.* The first word, "imperishable," means never to be overcome by an enemy. The second word, "uncorrupted," refers to a land that has not been polluted or defiled by a conquering army. The third word, "unfading," paints a picture of a land without change or decay. It refers especially to flowers that do not fade. *kept in heaven for you.* This inheritance is immune to disaster.

1:5 protected. Not only is the inheritance guarded and immune to disaster, but so too are the Christians for whom it exists. *salvation.* While Christ is the object of the believer's hope, salvation is the result.

1:6 for a short time you have had to be distressed. By these two clauses, Peter gives perspective to their suffering. First, it will be temporary ("for a short time"). Second, such trials are circumstantial, perhaps even necessary ("you have had to" or "it was necessary"). *trials.* Peter's first allusion to their persecution.

3:1 Wives, in the same way. By this phrase Peter makes a transition from slaves to wives. Just as the behavior of Christ was the model for slaves, so too is it for women. *submit yourselves.* Again, as he did for slaves, Peter counsels submission to husbands, not rebellion. *won over.* Peter (like Paul) does not counsel Christian women to leave unbelieving husbands. His desire is that the husbands be converted, perhaps by the example of their wives.

SESSION QUOTATIONS

1. John MacArthur, *Twelve Extraordinary Women* (Nashville, TN: Nelson books, 2005), p. 27.

Session Six

REQUIRED SUPPLIES AND PREPARATION FOR EACH SESSION

SESSION 1:

Name Acrostic ...

Supplies: - paper,
- pens, colored markers, and crayons

Procedure:

Instruct group members to write their first names vertically along the left margin on their sheets of paper. Using these letters ask each person to create an acrostic that describes her. For instance:

E nthusiastic about gardening
M other of four children
I nterested in politics and current events
L oves Italian food
Y earns to hike the Appalachian Trail

Allow group members to decorate their acrostics by drawing pictures that also identify something about themselves. Ask each group member to share her acrostic with the group.

Fragmented Vision ...

Supplies: - Bring a kaleidoscope to pass around during your discussion in the "Connecting " segment.

Before the meeting begins, set up a DVD player. Be sure to bring a DVD of the film, Groundhog Day, *which stars Bill Murray and Andie MacDowell. Read the following "Stuck in a Rut" introduction and then show the second half of Scene 21 "Phil kidnaps Phil" into the beginning of Scene 22 (start at 1:02:50 and watch to around 1:06:33 on the DVD timer). After viewing the scene together, discuss the following questions.*

SESSION 2:

Stuck in a Rut ...

Supplies: - Have a TV/DVD player set up
- *Groundhog Day* DVD (1993/2002 in DVD starring Bill Murray and Andie MacDowell)

Preparation

Procedure:
Read the "Stuck in a Rut" introductory paragraph and then show the second half of Scene 21 "Phil kidnaps Phil" into the beginning of Scene 22 (start at 1:02:50 and watch to around 1:06:33 on the DVD timer). After viewing the movie scene, discuss the related questions.

Redeeming Regrets ...

Supplies: - Several pre-cut strips of construction paper for each person
- A few staplers or rolls for tape for connecting paper chains
- Markers to write on paper strips

Procedure for the Participants:
(1) On each strip of paper handed out by your leader, write a déjà vu issue or sin (in action or attitude) with which you struggle. (2) After writing on a few strips of paper, loop and tape the strips together into a paper chain. (3) Then, take time in silent prayer to repent of each of these sins and ask for God's forgiveness and wisdom. Each time you pray over a link, break that link and throw it in the trash. (4) When everyone is finished with their chains, discuss how you felt during this activity.

SESSION 3:

Life's a Box of Chocolates ...

Supplies: - Have a TV/DVD player set up
- *Forrest Gump* DVD (1994 starring Tom Hanks and Sally Field)

Procedure:
Set up a DVD player before the meeting begins. Read the introduction and then show Scene 14, "Mama's Trip to Heaven," (on the DVD timer from 1:38:47 to about 1:43:00 where he says he cuts the grass free). Discuss the related questions.

Heart Shields ...

Supplies: - Paper shields cut prior to the meeting from construction paper or card stock
- Colored markers to write on shields

Procedure:
Pass around the paper shields and colored markers. Ask group members to read and meditate on Philippians 4:6-7. Then, on their shields, ask them to write a prayer to God that praises Him for His goodness and guidance and turns over their anxieties to Him.

Secondhand Rose ...

Supplies: - CD or MP3 player set up
- A recording or downloaded MP3 file of Barbara Streisand's classic song "Secondhand Rose"

Procedure:

If you can locate the song, play it for group members before discussing the "Breaking the Ice" questions.

While You Were Sleeping ...

Supplies: - Have a TV/DVD player set up
- *While You Were Sleeping* DVD (1995 starring Sandra Bullock and Bill Pullman)

Procedure:

Read the introduction before question 2, and then show Scene 19, "A Second Chance," (on the DVD timer from 1:25:53 to 1:31:05, ending with the words: "He didn't want me"). Discuss questions 2-5 as a group.

SESSION 5:

Stretching Creative Muscles ...

Procedure:

Allow group members about 5 minutes to work individually on the first set of "Breaking the Ice" questions. Draw the group back together to enable women to share their responses. This should be a fun way to launch into the discussion of emotions. Discuss the remaining questions as a group. The first questions involves this idea: "We're going to stretch our creative muscles today with a quick writing exercise. It involves using all five senses to describe various emotions."

Scratch-Art Question ...

Supplies: - Purchase some scratch-art paper from a local art supplier or by searching for "scratch-art paper" on the Internet. Crayola® has a similar product for children called Color Explosion™ or Discovery Paper.
- Secure pens or other utensils required to use the scratch-art paper that you find.

Preparation

Procedure:

Play worship music to create a pleasant setting for this exercise. For question 3, give each woman a piece of the scratch-art paper and a utensil or pen. Instruct each one to spend 5 minutes of quiet time with God to ask Him to show her how He has worked in her life through her most difficult times. Ask group members to draw a picture representing the answer to the question: *How has God worked through your life's most difficult times?*

Point out that underneath the black surface group members will discover a rainbow of colors emerging under the pressure of their utensils or pens. Ask them to consider how God's power of redemption compares to the colors emerging from the paper's surface.

Take a few minutes together to share your drawings and stories.

SESSION 6:

Living Water in the Desert Rose ...

Supplies: - CD player set up + Worship music CD for background music
- A large serving bowl + a water pitcher (filled with water)
- Broken construction paper chain
- Small bag of sand available at arts and crafts stores

Procedure:

PASS 1: As worship music plays quietly, pass around an empty serving bowl. As you hold the bowl, pray aloud: "Lord, help me to make sense of my barren times." Continue around the circle with each person taking a turn.

PASS 2: When the bowl gets back to you, place a broken construction-paper chain inside. This will symbolize the sins released in Session Two. When the bowl reaches each person, she should pray aloud: "Lord, help me to let go of my past failures."

PASS 3: When the bowl gets back to you, pour a bag of sand into it. Explain that this represents the desert that Hagar faced as well as the dry times in our relationships with God. When the bowl reaches each person, she should pray aloud: "Lord, help me stay faithful in my desert times and to turn to You."

PASS 4: For the fourth part of this activity, pass around a pitcher of water. When the pitcher reaches each person, she should touch the actual water, and pray aloud: "Thank you, Holy Spirit, that Your presence in my heart is like never-ending wellspring of water to my parched soul. Help me to drink deeply and often."

Following the exercise, invite the group to discuss thoughts and feelings.

Preparation

LEADING A SMALL GROUP

You will find a great deal of helpful information in this section that will be crucial for success as you lead your group.

Reading through this and utilizing the suggested principles and practices will greatly enhance the group experience. You need to accept the limitations of leadership. You cannot transform a life. You must lead your group to the Bible, the Holy Spirit, and the power of Christian community. By doing so your group will have all the tools necessary to draw closer to God and each other, and to experiencing heart transformation.

Make the following things available at each session:
- *Redeeming our Regrets* book for each attendee
- Bible for each attendee
- Snacks and refreshments
- Pens or pencils for each attendee

THE SETTING AND GENERAL TIPS:

1. Prepare for each meeting by reviewing the material, praying for each group member, asking the Holy Spirit to join you, and making Jesus the centerpiece of every experience.

2. Create the right environment by making sure chairs are arranged so each person can see the eyes of every other attendee. Set the room temperature at 69 degrees. If meeting in a home, make sure pets are in a location where they cannot interrupt the meeting. Request that cell phones are turned off unless someone is expecting an emergency call. Have music playing as people arrive (volume low enough for people to converse) and, if possible, burn a sweet-smelling candle.

3. Try to have soft drinks and coffee available for early arrivals.

4. Have someone with the spiritual gift of hospitality ready to make any new attendees feel welcome.

5. Be sure there is adequate lighting so that everyone can read without straining.

6. There are four types of questions used in each session: Observation (What is the passage telling us?), Interpretation (What does the passage mean?), Self-revelation (How am I doing in light of the truth unveiled?), and Application (Now that I know what I know, what will I

do to integrate this truth into my life?). You won't be able to use all the questions in each study, but be sure to use some from each.

7. Connect with group members away from group time. The amount of participation you have during your group meetings is directly related to the amount of time you connect with your group members away from the meeting time.

8. Don't get impatient about the depth of relationship group members are experiencing. Building real Christian Community takes time.

9. Be sure pens and/or pencils are available for attendees at each meeting.

10. Never ask someone to pray aloud without first getting their permission.

LEADING MEETINGS:

1. Before the icebreakers, do not say, "Now we're going to do an icebreaker." The meeting should feel like a conversation from beginning to end, not a classroom experience.

2. Be certain every member responds to the icebreaker questions. The goal is for every person to hear his or her own voice early in the meeting. People will then feel comfortable to converse later on. If members can't think of a response, let them know you'll come back to them after the others have spoken.

3. Remember, a great group leader talks less than 10% of the time. If you ask a question and no one answers, just wait. If you create an environment where you fill the gaps of silence, the group will quickly learn they needn't join you in the conversation.

4. Don't be hesitant to call people by name as you ask them to respond to questions or to give their opinions. Be sensitive, but engage everyone in the conversation.

5. Don't ask people to read aloud unless you have gotten their permission prior to the meeting. Feel free to ask for volunteers to read.

6. Watch your time. If discussion time is extending past the time limits suggested, offer to the option of pressing on into other discussions or continuing the current session into your next meeting. REMEMBER: People and their needs are always more important than completing all the questions.

Leading a Small Group

THE GROUP:

Each small group has it's own persona. Every group is made up of a unique set of personalities, backgrounds, and life experiences. This diversity creates a dynamic distinctive to that specific group of people. Embracing the unique character of your group and the individuals in that group is vital to group members experiencing all you're hoping for.

Treat each person as special, responsible, and valuable members of this Christian community. By doing so you'll bring out the best in each of them, thus creating a living, breathing, life-changing group dynamic.

YOU CAN HELP GROUP MEMBERS THROUGH ...

Support – Provide plenty of time for support among the group members. Encourage members to connect with each other between meetings when necessary.

Shared Feelings – Reassure the members that their feelings are very normal in a situation such as they are in. Encourage the members to share their feelings with one another.

Advice Giving – Avoid giving advice. Encourage cross-talk (members talking to each other), but limit advice giving. "Should" and "ought" to statements tend to increase the guilt the loss has already created.

Silence – Silence is not a problem. Even though it may seem awkward, silence is just a sign that people are not ready to talk. It DOES NOT mean they aren't thinking or feeling. If the silence needs to be broken, be sure you break it with the desire to move forward.

Prayer – Prayer is vital to personal and community growth. Starting and ending with prayer is important. However, people may need prayer in the middle of the session. Here's a way to know when the time is right to pray. If a member is sharing and you sense a need to pray, then begin to look for a place to add it.

GROUP COVENANT

As you begin this study, it is important that your group covenant together, agreeing to live out important group values. Once these values are agreed upon, your group will be on its way to experiencing true Christian community. It's very important that your group discuss these values — preferably as you begin this study. The first session would be most appropriate.

* **Priority:** While we are in this group, we will give the group meetings priority.

* **Participation:** Everyone is encouraged to participate and no one dominates.

* **Respect:** Everyone is given the right to his or her own opinions, and all questions are encouraged and respected.

* **Confidentiality:** Anything that is said in our meetings is never repeated outside the meeting without permission.

* **Life Change:** We will regularly assess our progress toward applying the "steps" to an amazing marriage. We will complete the "Taking it Home" activities to reinforce what we are learning and better integrate those lessons into our lives.

* **Care and Support:** Permission is given to call upon each other at any time, especially in times of crisis. The group will provide care for every member.

* **Accountability:** We agree to let the members of our group hold us accountable to commitments we make in whatever loving ways we decide upon. Unsolicited advice giving is not permitted.

* **Empty Chair:** Our group will work together to fill the empty chair with an unchurched person or couple.

* **Mission:** We agree as a group to reach out and invite others to join us and to work toward multiplication of our group to form new groups.

* **Ministry:** We will encourage one another to volunteer to serve in a ministry and to support missions work by giving financially and/or personally serving.

I agree to all of the above_____ **date:** _____

Welcome to Community!

Meeting together with a group of people to study God's Word and experience life together is an exciting adventure. A small group is … *a group of people unwilling to settle for anything less than redemptive community.*

Core Values

Community: God is relational, so He created us to live in relationship with Him and each other. Authentic community involves *sharing life together* and *connecting* on many levels with the people in our group.

Group Process: Developing authentic community requires a step-by-step process. It's a journey of sharing our stories with each other and learning together.

Stages of Development: Every healthy group goes through *various* stages as it matures over a period of months or years. We begin with the *birth* of a new group, deepen our relationships in the *growth* and *development* stages, and ultimately *multiply* to form other new groups.

Interactive Bible Study: God provided the Bible as an instruction manual of life. We need to deepen our understanding of God's Word. People learn and remember more as they wrestle with truth and learn from others. The process of Bible discovery and group interaction will enhance our growth.

Experiential Growth: The goal of studying the Bible together is not merely a quest for knowledge; this should result in real life change. Beyond solely reading, studying, and dissecting the Bible, being a disciple of Christ involves reunifying knowledge with experience. We do this by bringing our questions to God, opening a dialogue with our hearts (instead of killing our desires), and utilizing other ways to listen to God speak to us (group interaction, nature, art, movies, circumstances, etc.). Experiential growth is always grounded in the Bible as God's primary means of revelation and our ultimate truth-source.

The Power of God: Our processes and strategies will be ineffective unless we invite and embrace the presence and power of God. In order to experience community and growth, Jesus needs to be the centerpiece of our group experiences and the Holy Spirit must be at work.

Redemptive Community: Healing best happens within the context of community and in relationship. A key aspect of our spiritual development is seeing ourselves through the eyes of others, sharing our stories, and ultimately being set free from the secrets and the lies we embrace that enslave our souls.

Mission: God has invited us into a larger story with a great mission. It is a mission that involves setting captives free and healing the broken-hearted (Isaiah 61:1-2). However, we can only join in this mission to the degree that we've let Jesus bind up our wounds and set us free. As a group experiences true redemptive community, other people will be attracted to that group, and through that group to Jesus. We should be alert to inviting others while we maintain (and continue to fill) an "empty chair" in our meetings to remind us of others who need to encounter God and authentic Christian community.

STAGES OF GROUP LIFE

Each healthy small group will move through various stages as it matures. There is no prescribed time frame for moving through these stages because each group is unique.

Birth Stage: This is the time in which group members form relationships and begin to develop community.

Multiply Stage: The group begins the multiplication process. Members pray about their involvement in establishing new groups. The new groups begin the cycle again with the Birth Stage.

Growth Stage: Here the group members begin to care for one another as they learn what it means to apply what they have discovered through Bible study, shared experiences, worship, and prayer.

Develop Stage: The Bible study and shared experiences deepen while the group members develop their gifts and skills. The group explores ways to invite neighbors, friends, and coworkers to meetings.

Subgrouping: If you have more than 12 people at a meeting, Serendipity House recommends dividing into smaller subgroups after the "Breaking the Ice" segment. Ask one person to be the leader of each subgroup, following the "Leader" directions for the session. The Group Leader should bring the subgroups back together for the closing. Subgrouping is also very useful when more openness and intimacy is required. The "Connecting" segment in each session is a great time to divide into smaller groups of four to six people.

SHARING YOUR STORIES

The sessions in *Redeeming Our Regrets* are designed to help you share a little of your personal lives with the other people in your group as you learn to parent well. Through your time together, each member of the group is encouraged to move from low risk, less personal sharing to higher risk communication. Real community will not develop apart from increasing intimacy of the group over time.

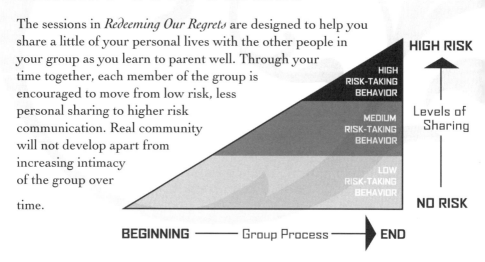

HIGH RISK

HIGH RISK-TAKING BEHAVIOR

MEDIUM RISK-TAKING BEHAVIOR

LOW RISK-TAKING BEHAVIOR

Levels of Sharing

NO RISK

BEGINNING —— Group Process —→ END

SHARING YOUR LIVES

As you share your lives together during this time, it is important to recognize that it is God who has brought each person to this group, gifting the individuals to play a vital role in the group (1 Corinthians 12:1). Each of you was uniquely designed to contribute in your own unique way to building into the lives of the other people in your group. As you get to know one another better, consider the following four areas that will be unique for each person. These areas will help you get a "grip" on how you can better support others and how they can support you.

G – Spiritual Gifts: God has given you unique spiritual gifts (1 Corinthians 12; Romans 12:3-8; Ephesians 4:1-16; etc.).

R – Resources: You have resources that perhaps only you can share, including skill, abilities, possessions, money, and time (Acts 2:44-47; Ecclesiastes 4:9-12, etc.).

I – Individual Experiences: You have past experiences, both good and bad, that God can use to strengthen others (2 Corinthians 1:3-7; Romans 8:28, etc.).

P – Passions: There are things that excite and motivate you. God has given you those desires and passions to use for His purposes (Psalm 37:4,23; Proverbs 3:5-6,13-18; etc.).

To better understand how a group should function and develop in these four areas, consider going through the Serendipity study entitled *Great Beginnings*.

GROUP MEETING STRUCTURE

Each of your group meetings will include a four-part agenda.

1. Breaking the Ice: This section includes fun, uplifting questions to warm up the group and help group members get to know one another better as they begin the journey of becoming a connected community. These questions prepare the group for meaningful discussion throughout the session.

2. Discovering the Truth: The heart of each session is the interactive Bible study time. The goal is for the group to discover biblical truths through open, discovery questions that lead to further investigation. The emphasis in this section is on understanding what the Bible says through interaction within your group.

To help the group experience a greater sense of community, it is important for everybody to participate in the "Discovering the Truth" and "Embracing the Truth" discussions. Even though people in a group have differing levels of biblical knowledge, it is vital that group members encourage each other to share what they are observing, thinking, and feeling about the Bible passages. Scripture notes are provided at the end of each session to provide additional Bible understanding.

3. Embracing the Truth: All study should direct group members to action and life change. This section continues the Bible study time but with an emphasis on leading the group members toward integrating the truths they have discovered into their lives. The questions are very practical and application-focused.

4. Connecting: One of the key goals of this study is to lead group members to grow closer to one another as the group develops a sense of community. This section focuses on further application, as well as opportunities for encouraging, supporting, and praying for one another. There are also opportunities to connect with God and to connect with your own heart.

BONUS – Taking it Home: Between each session, there is some homework for group members. This typically includes a question to take to God and a question to take to your heart. These experiences are designed to reinforce the content of the session and help group members deepen their spiritual life and walk with Jesus.

About the Authors

More than 30,000 people currently attend Fellowship churches that Gene and Elaine Getz have planted in the Dallas area, while more churches span the globe. Dr. Gene Getz is a pastor, seminary professor, host of the "Renewal" radio program, and author of more than 50 books, including *The Walk, The Measure of a Man,* and *Building Up One Another.* Gene and Elaine recently released a revision of their best-selling book *The Measure of a Woman.* Elaine is a wonderful wife, mother, and grandmother, with much to pass on to younger women. The couple resides in Plano, Texas.

Acknowledgments

We truly appreciate the effective partnership between my team at the Center for Church Renewal and the team at Serendipity House, as well as all of the individuals who contributed to this effort.

We are deeply indebted to Iva Morelli and Sue Mitchell for their invaluable assistance in so many details of this and other projects.

My good friends at Serendipity House Publishing have again done a wonderful job in every aspect of this Women of Purpose study. We especially want to thank …
- Publisher Ron Keck for his vision
- Contributing writers Angela Akers and Ben Colter for working to develop this content into a small-group experience
- Brian Marschall for art direction and cover design
- The team at Powell Creative for design and layout of the interior
- Bethany McShurley for editorial expertise
- Sarah Hogg for an eye for detail

Regal Books, friends and partners in ministry, have graciously granted permission to include some content from *The Measure of a Woman* in this Women of Purpose series.

About the Authors

MEETING PLANNER

The leader or facilitator of our group is _____ .
The apprentice facilitator for this group is _____ .

We will meet on the following dates and times:

	Date	Day	Time
Session 1	_____	_____	_____
Session 2	_____	_____	_____
Session 3	_____	_____	_____
Session 4	_____	_____	_____
Session 5	_____	_____	_____
Session 6	_____	_____	_____

We will meet at:

Session 1 _____
Session 2 _____
Session 3 _____
Session 4 _____
Session 5 _____
Session 6 _____

Childcare will be arranged by: Refreshments by:

	Childcare	Refreshments
Session 1	_____	_____
Session 2	_____	_____
Session 3	_____	_____
Session 4	_____	_____
Session 5	_____	_____
Session 6	_____	_____

Meeting Planner

103

GROUP DIRECTORY

Write your name on this page. Pass your books around and ask your group members to fill in their names and contact information in each other's books.

Your Name: _____

Name: _____   Name: _____
Address: _____   Address: _____
City: _____   City: _____
Zip Code: _____   Zip Code: _____
Home Phone: _____   Home Phone: _____
Mobile Phone: _____   Mobile Phone: _____
E-mail: _____   E-mail: _____

Name: _____   Name: _____
Address: _____   Address: _____
City: _____   City: _____
Zip Code: _____   Zip Code: _____
Home Phone: _____   Home Phone: _____
Mobile Phone: _____   Mobile Phone: _____
E-mail: _____   E-mail: _____

Name: _____   Name: _____
Address: _____   Address: _____
City: _____   City: _____
Zip Code: _____   Zip Code: _____
Home Phone: _____   Home Phone: _____
Mobile Phone: _____   Mobile Phone: _____
E-mail: _____   E-mail: _____

Name: _____   Name: _____
Address: _____   Address: _____
City: _____   City: _____
Zip Code: _____   Zip Code: _____
Home Phone: _____   Home Phone: _____
Mobile Phone: _____   Mobile Phone: _____
E-mail: _____   E-mail: _____

Name: _____   Name: _____
Address: _____   Address: _____
City: _____   City: _____
Zip Code: _____   Zip Code: _____
Home Phone: _____   Home Phone: _____
Mobile Phone: _____   Mobile Phone: _____
E-mail: _____   E-mail: _____

Name: _____   Name: _____
Address: _____   Address: _____
City: _____   City: _____
Zip Code: _____   Zip Code: _____
Home Phone: _____   Home Phone: _____
Mobile Phone: _____   Mobile Phone: _____
E-mail: _____   E-mail: _____

Group Directory